Food from Heaven

The Eucharist in Scripture

Food from Heaven

The Eucharist in Scripture

Jeanne Kun

The Word Among Us Press
9639 Doctor Perry Road
Ijamsville, Maryland 21754
www.wordamongus.org

ISBN 978-1-59325-096-6

Made and printed in the United States of America.

14 13 12 11 10   4 5 6 7 8

Text & Cover Design: David Crosson

Nihil Obstat: The Reverend Michael Morgan, Chancellor
             Censor Librorum
             November 28, 2006
Imprimatur: +Most Reverend Victor Galeone
             Bishop of Saint Augustine
             November 28, 2006

Library of Congress Cataloging-in-Publication Data

Kun, Jeanne, 1951-
  Food from heaven : the eucharist in scripture / Jeanne Kun.
    p. cm.
  Includes bibliographical references.
  ISBN 978-1-59325-096-6 (alk. paper)
  1. Lord's Supper--Catholic Church. 2. Lord's Supper--Biblical teaching. I. Title.
  BX2215.3.K86 2007
  234'.163--dc22
                                            2006034758

Contents

Welcome to The Word Among Us Keys to the Bible   6

Introduction   10
    Encountering Jesus in the Eucharist

Session 1: Manna in the Desert   16
    Bread from Heaven

Session 2: The Blood of the Covenant   30
    The Covenant of Our Redemption

Session 3: Jesus' Revelation   44
    "I Am the Living Bread"

Session 4: The Last Supper   58
    The Sacrament of Our Salvation

Session 5: The Crucifixion   72
    The Power of the Cross

Session 6: Emmaus Journey   86
    The Breaking of the Bread

Practical Pointers for Bible Discussion Groups   99

Sources and Acknowledgments   103

Welcome to
The Word Among Us
Keys to the Bible

Have you ever lost your keys? Everyone seems to have at least one "lost keys" story to tell. Maybe you had to break a window of your house or wait for the auto club to let you into your car. Whatever you had to do probably cost you—in time, energy, money, or all three. Keys are definitely important items to have on hand!

The guides in The Word Among Us Keys to the Bible series are meant to provide you with a handy set of keys that can "unlock" the treasures of the Scriptures for you. Scripture is God's living word. Within its pages we meet the Lord. So as we study and meditate on Scripture and unlock its many treasures, we discover the riches it contains—and in the process, we grow in intimacy with God.

Since 1982, *The Word Among Us* magazine has helped Catholics develop a deeper relationship with the Lord through daily meditations that bring the Scriptures to life. More than ever, Catholics today desire to read and pray with the Scriptures, and many have begun to form small faith-sharing groups to explore the Bible together.

We recently conducted a survey among our magazine readers to learn what they wanted in a Catholic Bible study. The many enthusiastic responses we received led us to create this new series. Readers told us they are looking for easy-to-understand, faith-filled materials that approach Scripture from a clearly Catholic perspective. Moreover, they want a Bible study that shows them how they can apply what they learn from Scripture to their everyday lives. And since most of our readers lead busy lives, they asked for sessions that they can complete in an hour or two.

On the basis of the survey results, we set out to design a simple, easy-to-use Bible study guide that is also challenging and thought provoking. We hope that this guide fulfills those admittedly ambitious goals. We are confident, however, that taking the time to go through this guide—whether by yourself, with a friend, or in a small group—will be a worthwhile endeavor that will bear fruit in your life.

Sometimes the riches contained in the Old and New Testaments can seem inaccessible, but we only need the right "key" to unlock them. In *Food from Heaven: The Eucharist in Scripture,* we will unlock texts from the New Testament as well as the Old that focus on the Eucharist or prefigure it. Exploring these passages and images can give us valuable insights into this great gift and mystery—insights that will move us to a greater love for Jesus present in the Eucharist and a more profound reverence for his body broken for us and his blood poured out for us.

How to Use the Guides in This Series

The study guides in the Keys to the Bible series are divided into six sessions that each deal with a particular aspect of the topic. Before starting the first session, take the time to read the introduction, which contains helpful background information on the Scripture texts to be studied. It will provide the foundation for the six sessions that follow. In this guide, the introduction examines the richness of the Eucharist to lead us to a deeper encounter with Jesus in the sacrament, while each session focuses on a specific aspect of its multiple meanings.

Whether you use this guide for personal reflection and study, as part of a faith-sharing group, or as an aid in your prayer time, be sure to begin each session with prayer. Ask God to open his word to you and speak to you personally. Read each Scripture passage slowly and carefully. Then, take as much time as you need to meditate on the passage and pursue any thoughts it brings to mind. When you are ready, move on to the accompanying commentary, which offers various insights into the text.

Two sets of questions are included in each session to help you "mine" the Scripture passage and discover its relevance to your life. Those under the heading "Understand!" focus on the text itself and help you grasp what it means. Occasionally a question allows for a variety of answers and is meant to help you explore the passage from several angles. "Grow!" questions are intended to elicit a personal response by helping you examine your life in light of the values and truths that you uncover through your study of the Scripture passage and its setting. Under the headings "Reflect!" and "Act!" we offer suggestions to help you respond concretely to the challenges posed by the passage.

Finally, pertinent quotations from the Fathers of the Church as well as insights from contemporary writers appear throughout each session. Coupled with relevant selections from the *Catechism of the Catholic Church* and information about the history, geography, and culture of first-century Palestine, these selections (called "In the Spotlight") add new layers of understanding and insight to your study.

As is true with any learning resource, you will benefit the most from this study by writing your answers to the questions in the spaces provided. The simple act of writing can help you formulate your thoughts more clearly—and will also give you a record of your reflections and spiritual growth that you can return to in the future to see how much God has accomplished in your life. End your reading or study with a prayer thanking God for what you have learned—and ask the Holy Spirit to guide you in living out the call you have been given as a Christian in the world today.

Although the Scripture passages to be studied and the related verses for your reflection are printed in full in each guide (from the New Revised Standard Version: Catholic Edition), you will find it helpful to have a Bible on hand for looking up other passages and cross-references or for comparing different translations.

The format of the guides in The Word Among Us Keys to the Bible series is especially well suited for use in small groups. Some recommendations and practical tips for using this guide in a Bible discussion group are offered on pages 99–102.

As you use this book to unlock the meaning of the Eucharist, may the Holy Spirit draw you closer to Jesus, increase your love for him, and strengthen your faith in his presence in this great sacrament.

The Word Among Us Press

Introduction

Encountering Jesus in the Eucharist

"Take and eat . . . take and drink." Simple words. A common invitation. Yet, Jesus was inviting his disciples to no ordinary meal. He said of the bread and wine that he offered them, "This is my body, . . . this is my blood" (Matthew 26:26, 28). Jesus' friends were invited to become partakers in his divine life by eating his flesh, the bread of life, and drinking his blood, the cup of salvation.

Since Jesus first spoke these words in Jerusalem on the eve of his death, they have been repeated millions of times, in every corner of the world, in every celebration of the Eucharist. And through two millennia, with awe and wonder and gratitude, we have contemplated the great gift that Jesus gave us and have sought to fathom its mystery.

The Eucharist in Scripture

Our primary understanding of the Eucharist is grounded in the accounts that Matthew, Mark, and Luke have handed down to us, which recount the words Jesus spoke and the actions he performed while at table with his closest followers on the night before he died. Describing that evening's meal, Luke tells us that Jesus "took a loaf of bread, and when he had given thanks, he broke it and gave it to them, saying, 'This is my body, which is given for you. Do this in remembrance of me.' And he did the same with the cup after supper, saying, 'This cup that is poured out for you is the new covenant in my blood'" (Luke 22:19-20; see also Matthew 26:26-28; Mark 14:22-24).

Jesus' institution of the Eucharist is familiar to us because we hear these same words and see these same actions repeated every time we attend Mass. Yet the Scriptures contain much more about the Eucharist than the synoptic gospels' accounts of the Last Supper. The Old Testament's record of the first stages of God's plan of salvation presents a variety of images that point to the fulfillment of this plan in Christ. Indeed, many of the realities described in the historical and prophetic books of the ancient Hebrew Scriptures—including persons, material objects, and events—anticipate or foreshadow, from the Christian perspective, greater realities that are made complete with the coming of Jesus or fully accomplished through his redemptive death and resurrection. Thus, the mystery of Christ that lies hidden in Old Testament "prefigurements" or "types" comes fully alive in the New.

In *Food from Heaven: The Eucharist in Scripture,* we will read and study passages from both the New and Old Testaments that will uncover for us the many layers of meaning to be found in the Eucharist and help us come to a more mature understanding and appreciation of it. In the first two chapters of this guide, we will explore two Old Testament occurrences that anticipate the Eucharist: the manna miraculously given to the Israelites to sustain them on their wilderness journey (Exodus 16) and the sealing of the Mosaic covenant with a blood sacrifice (Exodus 19 and 24). The next four chapters focus on passages in the gospels that unfold the Eucharist in its fullness and in which the eucharistic types of the Old Testament are fulfilled in the New: Jesus' declaration that he is the bread of life (John 6:35-69), the Last Supper (Luke 22:7-20), Jesus' crucifixion and atoning death (John 19), and Jesus' breaking of the bread with the two disciples in Emmaus (Luke 24:13-35). "Reflect!" sections include additional passages from the Hebrew prophets and the psalms as well as the Acts of the Apostles and the epistles. These texts particularly highlight the harmony between the Old and New Testaments and complement the specific topic presented in each session.

The Richness of the Eucharist

The revelation of Scripture and the truths it teaches about the Eucharist are reflected in many of the titles that have been given to it. Indeed, what the *Catechism of the Catholic Church* describes as the "inexhaustible richness of this sacrament" (1328) is especially apparent in the array of names by which the Eucharist is known, each one revealing and highlighting yet another of its wonders.

The Greek verb *eucharisteo* (used in Matthew 26:27 and Mark 14:23 to describe Jesus' action at the Last Supper) means "to give thanks" and particularly recalls the Jewish custom of offering a prayer—"the blessing"—over a meal to thank God for providing food for his people. In the offertory of the Mass, the celebrant blesses and thanks God, the Creator, for bread and wine, the gifts of his creation. Each of the eucharistic prayers includes praise and thanksgiving. In the celebration of Communion, we receive with gratitude the gift of Jesus' body and blood, thankful that through this gift we have been redeemed from sin and restored to the Father. Thus, the Liturgy of the Eucharist, as reflected by its name, is a supreme act of thanksgiving to God, a public acknowledgment and celebration of his divine goodness.

Since it constitutes a commemoration and re-presentation of Christ's sacrifice on Calvary, the sacrament is also called "the memorial of the Lord's passion and resurrection" and "the holy sacrifice." It is known, too, as "the Lord's Supper" and "the paschal banquet," names that remind us that Jesus first offered us the Eucharist at his last meal before his death and that at the end of time we will celebrate the marriage feast of the Lamb in the heavenly Jerusalem. That these particular names for the sacrament are based on biblical events points to the fact that teachings about the Eucharist are rooted in Scripture.

"Sacrifice of praise," "the sacrament of our salvation," "the true presence"—each of these other familiar titles focuses our vision on another luminous aspect of the richness of this sacrament.

The Body and Blood of Christ

The eucharistic celebration is first and foremost a meal. It was instituted by Christ at the final supper he shared with his apostles, and its elements consist of bread and wine—food and drink. But what makes this meal unique is that before he shared the bread and wine with his friends, Jesus transformed these elements into "living bread" and "the cup of eternal life"—his own body and blood that was to be shed for our salvation. Following Jesus' directive to "do this in remembrance of me," we re-create this first Eucharist at every celebration of the Mass. First, bread, "which earth has given and human hands have made," and wine, "fruit of the vine and work of human hands," are offered to God. Then, with the invocation of the Holy Spirit and Jesus' own words spoken now by the priest *in persona Christi*, bread and wine become Christ's body and blood.

Christ is mysteriously yet truly present to us in the Sacrament of the Eucharist. How the bread and wine become Christ's life-giving body and blood is a mystery that requires faith; it surpasses human understanding and cannot be grasped by our intellect or apprehended by our senses. As the church has ever believed and affirmed, "It is not man that causes the things offered to become the Body and Blood of Christ, but he who was crucified for us, Christ himself. The priest, in the role of Christ, pronounces these words, but their power and grace are God's. This is my body, he says. This word transforms the things offered" (CCC, 1375).

The Fruits of Holy Communion

Just as inexhaustible richness and a multiplicity of meanings are contained in the mystery of the Eucharist, so are its fruits equally rich and varied. The Eucharist has an inestimable power to work its effects on our heart and mind, on our body and soul and spirit, because Christ himself is alive within us: "Those who eat my flesh and drink my blood abide in me, and I in them" (John 6:56).

In receiving Communion, we *become* the very thing we *receive*. "Christ makes himself a transformative presence when we eat and drink him at communion," Bernardo Olivera explains. "We consume him in order to be converted into his own body; we assimilate him in order to be assimilated" (*The Search for God: Conferences, Letters, and Homilies*). Through the Eucharist we are united to Christ in a union that is not only spiritual but also physical: Christ is in us and we are in Christ. We consume Jesus, and he consumes us, enveloping us with his grace and empowering us to follow him.

Just as our physical body requires food to sustain life, our soul requires sustenance to maintain spiritual life. The Eucharist is our primary source of spiritual nourishment. Jesus told the crowd, "[M]y flesh is true food and my blood is true drink. . . . Those who eat my flesh and drink my blood have eternal life, and I will raise them up on the last day" (John 6:55, 54). This spiritual food also strengthens us to resist sin and temptation and helps us to grow in holiness and virtue.

God's love is revealed to us in the gift of the Eucharist; he sacrificed his only Son so that we might be reunited to him. That love flows into us when we share in the body and blood of Christ—and then flows through us to others. Christ's divine power enables us to love others as fully as we have been loved. And because Communion strengthens our union with Christ, it also strengthens our union and bonds of charity with one another and reinforces the unity of the church, the mystical body of Christ. Communion creates community. As we gather together for "the breaking of the bread," we are not only united more closely to Christ, we are united to one another—the other members of his body.

Finally, this wondrous sacrament renews our hope in the life to come: "Having passed from this world to the Father, Christ gives us in the Eucharist the pledge of glory with him. Participation in the Holy Sacrifice identifies us with his Heart, sustains our strength along the pilgrimage of this life, makes us long for eternal life, and unites us even now to the Church in heaven, the Blessed Virgin Mary, and all the saints" (CCC, 1419).

"Every fresh Communion is a new gift which Jesus Christ makes of himself," St. Ignatius of Loyola once said. As you progress through this guide, may your study, reflection, and prayer lead you into a deeper understanding of the gift and mystery of the Eucharist. And each time you receive Communion—"food from heaven"—may your love for Jesus grow greater and your union with him stronger.

Jeanne Kun

Bread from Heaven

Exodus 16:1-5, 13-26, 31, 35

¹ The whole congregation of the Israelites set out from Elim; and Israel came to the wilderness of Sin, which is between Elim and Sinai, on the fifteenth day of the second month after they had departed from the land of Egypt. ²The whole congregation of the Israelites complained against Moses and Aaron in the wilderness. ³The Israelites said to them, "If only we had died by the hand of the LORD in the land of Egypt, when we sat by the fleshpots and ate our fill of bread; for you have brought us out into this wilderness to kill this whole assembly with hunger."

⁴ Then the LORD said to Moses, "I am going to rain bread from heaven for you, and each day the people shall go out and gather enough for that day. In that way I will test them, whether they will follow my instruction or not. ⁵On the sixth day when they prepare what they bring in, it will be twice as much as they gather on other days."

¹³ [I]n the morning there was a layer of dew around the camp. ¹⁴When the layer of dew lifted, there on the surface of the wilderness was a fine flaky substance as fine as frost on the ground. ¹⁵When the Israelites saw it, they said to one another, "What is it?" For they did not know what it was. Moses said to them, "It is bread that the LORD has given you to eat. ¹⁶This is what the LORD has commanded: 'Gather as much of it as each of you needs, an omer to a person according to the number of persons, all providing for those in their own tents.'" ¹⁷The Israelites did so, some gathering more, some less. ¹⁸But when they measured it with an omer, those who gathered much had nothing over, and those who gathered little had no shortage; they gathered as much as each of them needed. ¹⁹And Moses said to them, "Let no one leave

> The sign of the manna was the proclamation of the coming of Christ who was to satisfy man's hunger for eternity by himself becoming the "living bread" which "gives life to the world."
> —**Pope John Paul II,** Homily at Wroclaw Cathedral, Poland

any of it over until morning." [20]But they did not listen to Moses; some left part of it until morning, and it bred worms and became foul. And Moses was angry with them. [21]Morning by morning they gathered it, as much as each needed; but when the sun grew hot, it melted.

[22] On the sixth day they gathered twice as much food, two omers apiece. When all the leaders of the congregation came and told Moses, [23]he said to them, "This is what the LORD has commanded: 'Tomorrow is a day of solemn rest, a holy sabbath to the LORD; bake what you want to bake and boil what you want to boil, and all that is left over put aside to be kept until morning.'" [24]So they put it aside until morning, as Moses commanded them; and it did not become foul, and there were no worms in it. [25]Moses said, "Eat it today, for today is a sabbath to the LORD; today you will not find it in the field. [26]Six days you shall gather it; but on the seventh day, which is a sabbath, there will be none."

[31] The house of Israel called it manna; it was like coriander seed, white, and the taste of it was like wafers made with honey. . . . [35]The Israelites ate manna forty years, until they came to a habitable land; they ate manna, until they came to the border of the land of Canaan.

God delivered the Israelites from their slavery in Egypt through the events recounted in the early chapters of the Book of Exodus. Yet they still had a lengthy way ahead of them before they would enter the promised land. Although this wilderness journey was not long in miles, it lasted forty years. During that time, God led his people through the desert by a pillar of cloud by day and fire by night (Exodus 13:21). When they cried out to him in hunger, he provided them with manna.

God told Moses that the Israelites were to gather a portion of manna each day, not leaving any over for the following day (Exodus 16:4, 19-21). In this way, they were challenged to actively rely on God for their "daily bread." On the sixth day of the week, however, the people were to collect a double portion, so that they could rest on the seventh day, the sabbath (16:22-26).

Some scholars seek an explanation for manna in nature, yet the Israelites recognized this strange substance as a gift from God—a supernatural phenomenon that expressed his generosity and his care for them. Extraordinary quantities of manna were continuously available to them except on the sabbath (Exodus 16:26)—a strange lack if the manna was simply a natural occurrence—and sustained them over quite a protracted duration of time. The Israelites received the manna as divine provision, bread rained down on them from heaven (16:4).

Manna was a foreshadowing of the Eucharist. Jesus himself compared the bread of the Eucharist to the manna given to the Israelites by God in the desert (John 6:32-33, 49-50, 58). In fact, many realities described in the Old Testament—persons, events, or other details—anticipate those fully revealed in the New. As the early Christians pondered the Scriptures, they realized that the ancient Israelites' record of the first stages of God's plan of salvation for human beings contained many images pointing to its fulfillment in Christ and recognized a harmony between the Old and New Testaments.

This understanding of the similitudes between the two testaments is called typology. The term "type" comes from the Greek word *tupos*, which means a blow or the mark or impression made by a blow. For example, a seal or signet ring leaves a "type" when pressed into soft wax. In theological language, a type is an image or imprint that points toward a greater reality—the true "prototype." A type is also known as a "figure" or "prefigurement," because it foreshadows or represents beforehand a future truth or reality.

As the *Catechism of the Catholic Church* explains, "'figures' (types) . . . announce [Christ] in the deeds, words, and symbols of the first covenant. By this re-reading in the Spirit of Truth, starting from Christ, the figures are unveiled" (1094). For example, the flood and Noah's ark, along with the crossing of the Red Sea, prefigured salvation by baptism. In the manna we recognize symbols of the Eucharist: God is with us, and he provides us with nourishment for our earthly journey—nourishment we can depend on each and every day.

Manna, mysterious bread from above, was also a symbol for God's word, supernatural food that gives life to the soul. As Moses exhorted the Israelites, "Remember the long way that the LORD your God has led you these forty years in the wilderness, in order to humble you, testing you to know what was in your heart, whether or not you would keep his commandments. He humbled you by letting you hunger, then by feeding you with manna . . . in order to make you understand that one does not live by bread alone, but by every word that comes from the mouth of the LORD" (Deuteronomy 8:2-3). Jesus, the Word-made-flesh, is the bread of God's word and the bread of the Eucharist: "The words that I have spoken to you are spirit and life" (John 6:63). For forty years, God fed his people in the desert. Through the paschal mystery, he now feeds us with himself. At each celebration of the Mass, we are richly fed, for "the Eucharistic table set for us is the table both of the Word of God and of the Body of the Lord" (CCC, 1346).

Understand!

1. Why did the Israelites complain after being delivered from their slavery in Egypt (Exodus 16:2-3)? In your opinion, what attitudes were underlying these complaints?

_____

_____

_____

_____

_____

_____

_____

2. How did God "test" the Israelites? Why? What do God's commands to his people indicate about what he expected of them? About what he highly values?

_____

_____

_____

_____

_____

_____

_____

3. What did the Israelites learn about God through their desert experience? What lessons did they also learn in the wilderness?

_____

_____

_____

_____

_____

_____

_____

4. In what ways was manna similar to the Eucharist? Also identify ways in which manna differed from the Eucharist.

_____

_____

_____

_____

_____

_____

_____

5. What does Moses' exhortation "One does not live by bread alone, but by every word that comes from the mouth of the LORD" (Deuteronomy 8:3) suggest about physical and spiritual hunger? About the effectiveness of God's word? About the importance of obeying God's word?

_____

_____

_____

_____

_____

_____

_____

▶ In the Spotlight
Food for the Journey

Centuries after God provided manna for the Israelties during their passage in the desert, he miraculously fed the prophet Elijah, who was on a similar journey. After Elijah fled from the idolatrous Queen Jezebel into the wilderness and lay down to rest, "suddenly an angel touched [Elijah] and said to him, 'Get up and eat.' He looked, and there at his head was a cake baked on hot stone, and a jar of water. . . . He got up, and ate and drank; then he went in the strength of that food forty days and forty nights to Horeb, the mount of God" (1 Kings 19:5-6, 8).

We too, like the Israelites and Elijah, are on a journey of faith. As St. Bede wrote, "The deliverance of the children of Israel and their journey to the long-promised land correspond with the mystery of our redemption. We are making our way toward the light of our heavenly home with the grace of Christ leading us and showing us the way." On our pilgrimage to heaven we are nourished and strengthened by the Eucharist—food from heaven, food for our journey to heaven.

Traditionally, the Eucharist is called "viaticum"—from the Latin, meaning "provision for a journey"—when it is received in the moments before death. "As the sacrament of Christ's Passover the Eucharist should always be the last sacrament of the earthly journey, the 'viaticum' for 'passing over' to eternal life" (CCC, 1517). The viaticum is "spiritual food by which we are sustained in our pilgrimage through this life, and also . . . paves our way to eternal glory and happiness" (*Catechism of the Council of Trent*).

Grow!

1. The Israelites longed for the security they had known in Egypt— forgetting the rigors of their bondage there—and feared the uncertainties they faced in the desert. Think of a time when you were reluctant to let go of what was familiar in order to allow God to direct your life. How did you deal with your feelings? How does this story of God's provision reassure you right now?

_____

_____

_____

_____

_____

_____

_____

2. When have you experienced God's caring for you in a crisis or filling a significant lack? How did he meet your need? What was your response?

_____

_____

_____

_____

_____

_____

_____

3. What is the greatest hunger in your life? How do you seek to satisfy it? How conscious are you of hungering after the Eucharist and drawing strength and nourishment from it?

_____

_____

_____

_____

_____

_____

_____

4. In what ways do you "live" by God's word (Deuteronomy 8:3)? How do you "feed" on it?

_____

_____

_____

_____

_____

_____

_____

5. St. Paul told the early Christian believers in Corinth that the Israelites' wilderness experiences "happened to them to serve as an example, and they were written down to instruct us" (1 Corinthians 10:11). What lesson have you learned from this study session to help you on your faith journey through life?

_____

_____

_____

_____

_____

_____

_____

▶ In the Spotlight
In the Words of the Saints

When the body is deprived of food it languishes and dies; and it is the same with the soul, without the Bread which sustains life.
—St. Theophane Vénard

Every day we ask God for the bread to sustain the life of our body. So, too, we have need of heavenly Bread that gives life to our soul. My advice is that you receive holy communion frequently—if you cannot do so daily—and unite yourself to the Savior.
—St. Pius X

Communion is the life of your soul. If you were to eat only one meal each week, would you survive? It's the same thing with your soul: You must nourish your soul with the Holy Eucharist. There is a beautiful table set up in front of us, with great food on it. But sometimes we don't even bother to take it!
—Blessed André Bessette

Reflect!

1. Meditate on these words from the Our Father: "Give us this day our daily bread" (Matthew 6:11).

   Do you find it difficult to trust God for daily necessities? If so, why? What particular need would you like God to meet today?

2. Read and reflect on the following passages to deepen your understanding of manna as a "type" for Jesus' body given to us in the Eucharist:

   > While the Israelites were camped in Gilgal [after crossing the Jordan River and entering into the promised land] they kept the passover in the evening on the fourteenth day of the month in the plains of Jericho. On the day after the passover, on that very day, they ate the produce of the land, unleavened cakes and parched grain. The manna ceased on the day they ate the produce of the land, and the Israelites no longer had manna; they ate the crops of the land of Canaan that year.
   > —Joshua 5:10-12

   > [H]e commanded the skies above,
   >   and opened the doors of heaven;
   > he rained down on them manna to eat,
   >   and gave them the grain of heaven,
   > Mortals ate of the bread of angels;
   >   he sent them food in abundance.
   > —Psalm 78:23-25

[Y]ou gave your people food of angels,
and without their toil you supplied them from heaven
    with bread ready to eat,
providing every pleasure and suited to every taste.
For your sustenance manifested your sweetness toward
    your children;
and the bread, ministering to the desire of the one
    who took it,
was changed to suit everyone's liking.

—Wisdom 16:20-21

So [the crowd] said to [Jesus], "What sign are you going to give us then, so that we may see it and believe you? What work are you performing? Our ancestors ate the manna in the wilderness; as it is written, 'He gave them bread from heaven to eat.'" Then Jesus said to them, "Very truly, I tell you, it was not Moses who gave you the bread from heaven, but it is my Father who gives you the true bread from heaven. For the bread of God is that which comes down from heaven and gives life to the world." They said to him, "Sir, give us this bread always." Jesus said to them, "I am the bread of life. Whoever comes to me will never be hungry, and whoever believes in me will never be thirsty."

—John 6:30-35

▶ In the Spotlight
"What Is It?"

"Manna" is the name given to the mysterious bread from heaven in Greek and English translations of Scripture. According to popular etymology, the origin of the word "manna" is explained by the question the puzzled Israelites asked in Exodus 16:15—"What is it?"—which in Hebrew sounds like *man hu*. But linguists have also suggested that the word's root may not be in an interrogative, but in an Egyptian expression for some kind of baked cake (see Numbers 11:7-8), borrowed into Hebrew when the Israelites said of this strange substance, "It is *man*."

Some scientists and scholars identify the biblical manna with the sticky, sweet resin exuded by the tamarisk (*tamarix mannifera*), a shrub that grows in mountains of the Sinai Peninsula, or with the secretions of certain insects that feed on the tamarisk sap or fruit and turn it into a fructose product similar to honey. The droplets of tamarisk resin or insect secretions crystallize in the cold night air and fall to the ground. Desert bedouins collect this substance—which even today they call *mann* in Arabic—in the early morning before it melts under the hot sun to suck or use as a sweetener in confections. However, it is quite unlikely that this substance, dependent on certain weather conditions and normally rather sparse, could have been available naturally and regularly to the ancient Israelites in such quantities as described in Exodus 16. It is equally unlikely that it would appear every day except the sabbath.

Act!

"When they measured [the manna] with an omer, those who gathered much had nothing over, and those who gathered little had no shortage; they gathered as much as each of them needed" (Exodus 16:18).

Don't "store up" more than you need. Share what God has generously given you with others. This week invite an elderly neighbor to dinner, contribute to your local food bank, give alms to support the work of a mission society, or donate clothing and household goods you no longer use to a charitable organization.

▶ In the Spotlight
Wisdom from the Church Fathers

This is our daily Bread; take it daily, that it may profit you daily. Live, as to deserve to receive it daily.
—St. Augustine

Consider now which is more excellent: the bread of angels or the flesh of Christ, which is indeed the body that gives life. The first was manna from heaven, the second is above the heavens. One was of heaven, the other is of the Lord of the heavens; one subject to corruption if it was kept till the morrow, the other free from all corruption, for if anyone tastes of it with reverence he will be incapable of corruption. . . . What happened in symbol is now fulfilled in reality.

If what you marvel at is a shadow, how great is the reality whose very shadow you marvel at. . . . You know now what is more excellent: light is preferable to its shadow, reality to its symbol, the body of the Giver to the manna he gave from heaven.
—St. Ambrose

The Covenant of Our Redemption

Exodus 19:3-6; 24:3-11

^{19:3}The LORD called to [Moses] from the mountain, saying, "Thus you shall say to the house of Jacob, and tell the Israelites: ⁴You have seen what I did to the Egyptians, and how I bore you on eagles' wings and brought you to myself. ⁵Now therefore, if you obey my voice and keep my covenant, you shall be my treasured possession out of all the peoples. Indeed, the whole earth is mine, ⁶but you shall be for me a priestly kingdom and a holy nation. These are the words that you shall speak to the Israelites."

^{24:3}Moses came and told the people all the words of the LORD and all the ordinances; and all the people answered with one voice, and said, "All the words that the LORD has spoken we will do." ⁴And Moses wrote down all the words of the LORD. He rose early in the morning, and built an altar at the foot of the mountain, and set up twelve pillars, corresponding to the twelve tribes of Israel. ⁵He sent young men of the people of Israel, who offered burnt offerings and sacrificed oxen as offerings of well-being to the LORD. ⁶Moses took half of the blood and put it in basins, and half of the blood he dashed against the altar. ⁷Then he took the book of the covenant, and read it in the hearing of the people;

> At the words of consecration, with all your heart and soul, renew "the new and everlasting covenant" between Jesus Christ and yourself by the mingling of your blood with his.
> —**Cardinal Francis Xavier Nguyen Van Thuan**, *The Road of Hope: A Gospel from Prison*

and they said, "All that the LORD has spoken we will do, and we will be obedient." ⁸Moses took the blood and dashed it on the people, and said, "See the blood of the covenant that the LORD has made with you in accordance with all these words."

⁹ Then Moses and Aaron, Nadab, and Abihu, and seventy of the elders of Israel went up, ¹⁰and they saw the God of Israel. Under his feet there was something like a pavement of sapphire stone, like the very heaven for clearness. ¹¹God did not lay his hand on the chief men of the people of Israel; also they beheld God, and they ate and drank.

In ancient times, people entered into a covenant to acknowledge a solemn and binding agreement. For example, nations formed alliances with one another by treaties or covenants, and a king and his subjects were bound together by a covenant. In the covenant that God made with the Israelites at Mount Sinai, he promised his faithfulness to them, making them his "treasured possession," "a priestly kingdom and a holy nation" (Exodus 19:5, 6). He pledged himself to protect his chosen people and establish them in a land of their own. The Israelites, for their part, promised to obey God's commandments. This solemn agreement was sealed by pouring out the blood of an ox onto the altar as a sacrificial offering and by sprinkling the blood on the people (24:5-8).

For the Israelites, blood was an apt symbol of the binding nature of the Mosaic covenant. They looked upon blood as sacred because they recognized that life depends on it—"For the life of every creature—its blood is its life" (Leviticus 17:14). Human beings and animals cannot live without blood circulating through the body. Moreover, blood was so sacred that it was offered to make atonement for sin: "For the life of the flesh is in the blood; and I have given it to you for making atonement for your lives on the altar" (17:11; see also 16:11-19). The blood of the animal sacrifice was a substitution for the blood of the one making the offering; the blood of the sacrifice was poured out to acknowledge the penalty due for sin. Finally, blood was believed to cleanse. The author of Hebrews writes that "when every commandment had been told to all the people by Moses in accordance with the law, he took the blood of calves and goats, . . . and sprinkled both the scroll itself and all the people. . . . Indeed, under the law almost everything is purified with blood, and without the shedding of blood there is no forgiveness of sins" (Hebrews 9:19, 22). Thus, the Israelites pledged their lives to God and were cleansed of their sin when they ratified the covenant with blood—both the source of life and means of atonement.

The covenant made at Mount Sinai was sealed with the blood of animals, blood that was a mere symbol of the life of those who offered it. The new covenant—the covenant of our redemption—has been sealed by the blood of Christ himself: "[I]f the blood of goats and bulls . . . sanctifies those who have been defiled so that their flesh is purified, how much more will the blood of Christ, who through the eternal Spirit offered himself without blemish to God, purify our conscience from dead works to worship the living God!" (Hebrews 9:13-14). Jesus offered his blood for us on the cross "once for all . . . to remove sin by the sacrifice of himself" (9:26). It is through the shedding of his blood that Jesus offers us the life he shares with the Father. It is through his atoning death that we have access to God himself. And it is through the Eucharist that we become participants in Jesus' sacrifice and receive the gift of salvation.

The ceremony sealing the covenant at Mount Sinai included the reading of the law to the Israelites as they were assembled together (Exodus 24:7), the offering of a sacrifice (24:5), and the holy meal that Moses and the elders later ate before God when they ascended the mountain (24:11). This sequence of events parallels the actions of the Mass: the reading of the word, the offertory and consecration, and Communion. The words that Moses spoke—"See the blood of the covenant that the Lord has made with you" (Exodus 24:8)—foreshadow Jesus' own words at the Last Supper, "[T]his is my blood of the covenant, which is poured out for many for the forgiveness of sins" (Matthew 26:28; see also Mark 14:24; Luke 22:20). Moses served as the mediator between God and the Israelite people; Jesus is the mediator of a new covenant (Hebrews 9:15; 12:24). In every celebration of the Mass, "It is Christ himself, the eternal high priest of the New Covenant who, acting through the ministry of the priests, offers the Eucharistic sacrifice. And it is the same Christ, really present under the species of bread and wine, who is the offering of the Eucharistic sacrifice" (*Catechism of the Catholic Church*, 1410).

Understand!

1. Why, in your opinion, did God remind Moses and the Israelites of all that he had done for them (see Exodus 19:4) before offering the covenant to them?

   _____

   _____

   _____

   _____

   _____

   _____

   _____

2. What did God promise to do in the covenant he made with the Israelites at Mount Sinai? What does this indicate about the nature of God? What did God require of the Israelites in the Mosaic covenant? How did they show their acceptance of the covenant God offered them?

   _____

   _____

   _____

   _____

   _____

   _____

   _____

3. Describe Moses' role in the covenant-making ceremony. What similarities between Moses and Jesus do you see in this text? What differences?

   _____

   _____

   _____

   _____

_____

_____

_____

4. What insights does the ritual sealing of this covenant give you
   into the significance of blood? Into the sacrificial nature of the
   Eucharist and the Mass?

_____

_____

_____

_____

_____

_____

5. What did the pouring out of the blood on the altar symbolize to
   the Israelites? Why was the blood also sprinkled on the people?

_____

_____

_____

_____

_____

▶ In the Spotlight
Mount Sinai, Mountain of God

The Sinai Peninsula, where the Israelites wandered thirty-three
centuries ago, has been called the meeting point of continents
and the dividing line between waters, the gateway from Africa
to Asia and the bridge between the Mediterranean and the
Red seas.

It was at Mount Sinai, in the rugged highlands of this desert peninsula, that Yahweh first appeared to Moses in the burning bush. And it was to this same mountain that Moses led the Israelites after their deliverance from Egypt. There God gave Moses the Ten Commandments, and entered into a covenant with the Israelites.

Mount Sinai has traditionally been identified with Jebel Mûsa, an imposing red granite peak rising 2,600 feet above the Sinai plateau. It lies in a stark and barren mountain ridge fifty-five miles north of the southern tip of the triangular peninsula. From the third century onward, monks settled in caves around this holy site, and the Monastery of St. Catherine—built in the sixth century during the reign of the Byzantine emperor Justinian—has stood at the foot of Mount Sinai for more than 1,400 years.

Some scholars propose that the name "Sinai" is derived from the Semitic *sen*, meaning "tooth," because of the jagged shape of the mountain; others suggest that the word derives from Sin, the moon goddess worshipped by the earliest inhabitants of the region.

Grow!

1. Through Jesus' sacrificial death—in which he shed his blood—we receive salvation: "In him we have redemption through his blood" (Ephesians 1:7). What does redemption mean to you? What is your personal experience of being redeemed?

_____

_____

_____

_____

_____

_____

2. How is your relationship with God like a covenant? What promises has God made to you? What covenant promises or solemn commitments have you made to him? How does the Eucharist help you live out these promises?

_____

_____

_____

_____

_____

_____

_____

3. What other covenant relationships have you entered into—for example, marriage or a business contract? What obligations and responsibilities are involved in these agreements? What do these covenants teach you about your covenant with God?

_____

_____

_____

_____

_____

_____

_____

4. Moses served as the mediator between God and the Israelite people; Jesus is the mediator of a new covenant (Hebrews 9:15; 12:24). Think of an occasion when you acted as a mediator between two people. What did you learn from this experience?

_____

_____

_____

_____

_____

_____

5. "The blood of Jesus . . . cleanses us from all sin" (1 John 1:7). In what specific areas of your life have you experienced this cleansing? Write a prayer thanking Jesus for forgiving your sins and for offering you a share in divine life through the Eucharist.

_____

_____

_____

_____

_____

_____

_____

▶ In the Spotlight
In the Words of the Saints

That in this sacrament are the true Body of Christ and his true Blood is something that cannot be apprehended by the senses but only by faith, which relies on divine authority.
—St. Thomas Aquinas

Upon receiving Holy Communion, the adorable blood of Jesus Christ flows in our veins and his flesh is really blended with ours.
—St. John Vianney

Reflect!

1. Reflect on Romans 3:23-25: "[A]ll have sinned and fall short of the glory of God; they are now justified by his grace as a gift, through the redemption that is in Christ Jesus, whom God put forward as a sacrifice of atonement by his blood, effective through faith."

   Ask the Holy Spirit to help you make an examination of conscience. Then express to God your sorrow for your sins in an act of contrition. Finally, express your gratitude for Jesus' sacrifice of atonement and the redemption and forgiveness you have through him. If possible, receive the Sacrament of Reconciliation this week.

2. Read and reflect on the following passages to enhance your understanding of Christ's atoning sacrifice offered for us:

   > The LORD summoned Moses and spoke to him from the tent of meeting, saying: Speak to the people of Israel and say to them: When any of you bring an offering of livestock to the LORD, you shall bring your offering from the herd or from the flock. If the offering is a burnt offering from the herd, you shall offer a male without blemish; you shall bring it to the entrance of the tent of meeting, for acceptance in your behalf before the LORD. You shall lay your hand on the head of the burnt offering, and it shall be acceptable in your behalf as atonement for you. The bull shall be slaughtered before the LORD; and Aaron's sons the priests shall offer the blood, dashing the blood against all sides of the altar that is at the entrance of the tent of meeting. . . . Then the priest shall turn the whole into smoke on the altar as a burnt offering, an offering by fire of pleasing odor to the LORD.
   >
   > —Leviticus 1:1-5, 9

[Christ] entered once for all into the Holy Place, not with the blood of goats and calves, but with his own blood, thus obtaining eternal redemption. . . . For this reason he is the mediator of a new covenant, so that those who are called may receive the promised eternal inheritance, because a death has occurred that redeems them from the transgressions under the first covenant.

—Hebrews 9:12, 15

Christ did not enter a sanctuary made by human hands, a mere copy of the true one, but he entered into heaven itself, now to appear in the presence of God on our behalf. Nor was it to offer himself again and again, as the high priest enters the Holy Place year after year with blood that is not his own; for then he would have had to suffer again and again since the foundation of the world. But as it is, he has appeared once for all at the end of the age to remove sin by the sacrifice of himself. And just as it is appointed for mortals to die once, and after that the judgment, so Christ, having been offered once to bear the sins of many, will appear a second time, not to deal with sin, but to save those who are eagerly waiting for him.

—Hebrews 9:24-28

[E]very priest stands day after day at his service, offering again and again the same sacrifices that can never take away sins. But when Christ had offered for all time a single sacrifice for sins, "he sat down at the right hand of God," and since then has been waiting "until his enemies would be made a footstool for his feet." For by a single offering he has perfected for all time those who are sanctified.

—Hebrews 10:11-14

▶ In the Spotlight
The Meaning of the Mass

American Jesuit priest Walter Ciszek was captured by the Russian Army during World War II and was convicted of being a "Vatican spy." He spent fourteen years in Soviet prisons and the labor camps of Siberia, and was forced to live ten more years in Siberia. He was exchanged for a Soviet spy arrested in the United States and returned to the United States in 1963.

When I reached the prison camps of Siberia, I learned to my great joy that it was possible to say Mass daily once again. In every camp, the priests and prisoners would go to great lengths, run risks willingly, just to have the consolation of this sacrament. For those who could not get to Mass, we daily consecrated hosts and arranged for the distribution of Communion to those who wished to receive. Our risk of discovery, of course, was greater in the barracks, because of the lack of privacy and the presence of informers. Most often, therefore, we said our daily Mass somewhere at the work site during the noon break. Despite this added hardship, everyone observed a strict Eucharistic fast from the night before, passing up a chance for breakfast and working all the morning on an empty stomach. Yet no one complained. In small groups the prisoners would shuffle into the assigned place, and there the priest would say Mass in his working clothes, unwashed, disheveled, bundled up against the cold. We said Mass in drafty storage shacks, or huddled in mud and slush in the corner of a building site foundation of an underground. The intensity of devotion of both priests and prisoners made up for everything; there were no altars, candles, bells, flowers, music, snow-white linens, stained glass or the warmth that even the simplest parish church could offer. Yet in these primitive conditions, the Mass brought you closer to God than anyone might conceivably imagine. The realization of what was happening on the board, box, or stone used in place of an altar penetrated deep into the soul. Distractions caused by the fear of discovery, which accompanied each saying of the Mass under such conditions, took nothing away from the effect that the tiny bit of bread and a few drops of consecrated wine produced upon the soul.

—Walter J. Ciszek, SJ

Act!

The Anima Christi is a prayer that originated in the early part of the fourteenth century. St. Ignatius of Loyola (1491–1556) later recommended its use in his Spiritual Exercises.

This week pray this prayer in thanksgiving after receiving Communion. Note especially its references to the effects of Christ's body and blood offered for us:

Soul of Christ, sanctify me.
Body of Christ, save me.
Blood of Christ, inebriate me.
Water from the side of Christ, wash me.
Passion of Christ, strengthen me.
O good Jesus, hear me.
Within your wounds hide me.
Do not allow me to be separated from you.
From the malevolent enemy defend me.
In the hour of my death, call me,
and bid me come to you,
that with your saints I may praise you.
forever and ever.
Amen.

▶ In the Spotlight
Wisdom from the Church Fathers

If as often as the Lord's blood is shed, it is poured forth for the remission of sins, I ought to receive it always, so that my sins may always be forgiven. I who am always committing sin ought always to have a remedy.
—**St. Ambrose**

When, therefore, we eat the holy flesh of Christ, the Savior of us all, and drink his precious blood, we have life in us, being made as it were, one with him, and abiding in him, and possessing him also in us.
—**St. Cyril of Alexandria**

"I Am the Living Bread"

John 6:35-69

35 Jesus said to [the crowd who followed him after the multiplication of the loaves and fish], "I am the bread of life. Whoever comes to me will never be hungry, and whoever believes in me will never be thirsty. 36But I said to you that you have seen me and yet do not believe. 37Everything that the Father gives me will come to me, and anyone who comes to me I will never drive away; 38for I have come down from heaven, not to do my own will, but the will of him who sent me. 39And this is the will of him who sent me, that I should lose nothing of all that he has given me, but raise it up on the last day. 40This is indeed the will of my Father, that all who see the Son and believe in him may have eternal life and I will raise them up on the last day."

> I want the bread of God, which is the flesh of Jesus Christ, . . . and for drink I want his blood, the sign of his imperishable love.
>
> —St. Ignatius of Antioch, *Letter to the Romans*

41 Then the Jews began to complain about him because he said, "I am the bread that came down from heaven." 42They were saying, "Is not this Jesus, the son of Joseph, whose father and mother we know? How can he now say, 'I have come down from heaven'?" 43Jesus answered them, "Do not complain among yourselves. 44No one can come to me unless drawn by the Father who sent me; and I will raise that person up on the last day. 45It is written in the prophets, 'And they shall all be taught by God.' Everyone who has heard and learned from the Father comes to me. 46Not that anyone has seen the Father except the one who is from God; he has seen the Father. 47Very truly, I tell you, whoever believes has eternal life. 48I am the bread of life. 49Your ancestors ate the manna in the wilderness, and they died. 50This is the bread that comes down from heaven, so that one may eat of it and not die. 51I am the living bread that came down from heaven. Whoever eats of this bread will live forever; and the bread that I will give for the life of the world is my flesh."

⁵² The Jews then disputed among themselves, saying, "How can this man give us his flesh to eat?" ⁵³So Jesus said to them, "Very truly, I tell you, unless you eat the flesh of the Son of Man and drink his blood, you have no life in you. ⁵⁴Those who eat my flesh and drink my blood have eternal life, and I will raise them up on the last day; ⁵⁵for my flesh is true food and my blood is true drink. ⁵⁶Those who eat my flesh and drink my blood abide in me, and I in them. ⁵⁷Just as the living Father sent me, and I live because of the Father, so whoever eats me will live because of me. ⁵⁸This is the bread that came down from heaven, not like that which your ancestors ate, and they died. But the one who eats this bread will live forever." ⁵⁹He said these things while he was teaching in the synagogue at Capernaum.

⁶⁰ When many of his disciples heard it, they said, "This teaching is difficult; who can accept it?" ⁶¹But Jesus, being aware that his disciples were complaining about it, said to them, "Does this offend you? ⁶²Then what if you were to see the Son of Man ascending to where he was before? ⁶³It is the spirit that gives life; the flesh is useless. The words that I have spoken to you are spirit and life. ⁶⁴But among you there are some who know and do not believe." For Jesus knew from the first who were the ones that did not believe, and who was the one that would betray him.

⁶⁶ Because of this many of his disciples turned back and no longer went about with him. ⁶⁷So Jesus asked the twelve, "Do you also wish to go away?" ⁶⁸Simon Peter answered him, "Lord, to whom can we go? You have the words of eternal life. ⁶⁹We have come to believe and know that you are the Holy One of God."

To those who followed him after they had eaten their fill of the loaves (John 6:22-24), Jesus made some startling declarations: "I am the bread of life. Whoever comes to me will never be hungry, and whoever believes in me will never be thirsty. . . . I am the living bread that came down from heaven. Whoever eats of this bread will live forever; and the bread that I will give for the life of the world is my flesh" (6:35, 51).

Jesus' earlier actions anticipate his gift of his own body and blood for our food. His very first miracle—transforming water into wine at the wedding in Cana—prefigures the transformation of wine into his blood in the Eucharist. And in feeding the crowd that had gathered near the Sea of Galilee with the five barley loaves and two fish, Jesus performed the same actions that he would later perform at the Last Supper: "Jesus took the loaves, and when he had given thanks, he distributed them" (John 6:11). Even Jesus' lying in a manger—an animals' feedbox—at his birth seems to foreshadow this miraculous gift of himself.

> When we partake of the Eucharist, we enter into a life-giving relationship with Jesus and the Father.

Jesus applies God's own name—"I AM" (Exodus 3:14)—to himself, for he is the Word made flesh, God's presence in the world. Many in the crowd complained, wondering how a man they had known all their lives and his—the neighbor boy, son of the local carpenter—could make such claims (John 6:41-42). Jesus confronted their unbelief (6:36) by inviting them to faith in him as the one sent by the Father and assuring them that "whoever believes has eternal life" (6:47).

To believe in Jesus and accept the revelation he brings means to recognize that he has come from God (John 6:38, 42, 50). And it is because he has come from God that he can reveal God to us (6:46). Indeed, to believe that Jesus of Nazareth is who he says he is—the Word made flesh, the Son of God who fulfills his Father's work of giving life—is the heart of our Christian faith. And this faith is itself a gift from God: "This is indeed the will of my Father, that all who see the Son and believe in him may have eternal life" (6:40).

To Jesus' listeners—Jews forbidden to consume even the blood of animals as food (Leviticus 17:14)—his words sounded not only mystifying but appalling: "Unless you eat the flesh of the Son of Man and drink his blood, you have no life in you. Those who eat my flesh and drink my blood have eternal life, . . . for my flesh is true food and my blood is true drink. Those who eat my flesh and drink my blood abide in me, and I in them" (John 6:53-56). Yet in the Eucharist Jesus fulfilled these remarkable claims, giving us himself—his flesh and blood—through the miraculous transubstantiation of bread and wine. When we partake of it, we enter into a life-giving relationship with him and the Father.

Many who heard Jesus' "difficult" teaching were not only mystified but scandalized, and they turned away from him (John 6:60, 66). "Do you also wish to go away?" (6:67) Jesus asked the twelve, his closest friends. "The Lord's question echoes through the ages, as a loving invitation to discover that only he has 'the words of eternal life' and that to receive in faith the gift of his Eucharist is to receive the Lord himself" (*Catechism of the Catholic Church,* 1336). May we, like Peter, answer wholeheartedly, "Lord, to whom can we go? You have the words of eternal life. We have come to believe and know that you are the Holy One of God" (6:69).

Understand!

1. Note all the descriptive phrases Jesus used to speak of himself in John 6:35-58. What promises are connected with these descriptions?

   I am the bread of life - You will never be hungry
   I am the living bread - You'll never be thirsty
   My Flesh is true food my blood is true drink
   My words are spirit and life
   Whoever comes to me will live
   forever.

2. How does the "living bread"—Jesus' own flesh given to us in the Eucharist—differ from the manna described in Exodus 16 and John 6:49, 58?

   They ate it -- and died
   Physical sustainance only
   His living bread will allow
   us to live forever

3. What did Jesus say about belief and faith in his discourse with the Jews? Why is it so important to believe in him?

   His words are Spirit and life.

   This is the will of my
   Father.

4. According to Jesus' teaching, what are the consequences if one does not eat his flesh or drink his blood?

You will have no life in you.

5. How do you think that the crowd—who knew nothing about the Eucharist or Jesus' passion—would have interpreted Jesus' claim that they must eat his body and drink his blood? Why do you think Jesus didn't offer any more of an explanation?

So their spirits would stir in them and have faith

▶ In the Spotlight
The Eucharist Is Always a Miracle

About six hundred boys were present in church. The ciborium in the tabernacle was almost empty, containing at most twenty particles. The sexton had prepared another ciborium for consecration, but at the last moment forgot all about it and left it in the sacristy. At communion time, when Don Bosco uncovered the ciborium he had taken from the tabernacle and noticed its contents, a look of distress came over his face. The altar boys noticed that he raised his eyes to heaven in mute supplication and then went down to give communion to the first row. But one row succeeded another, and still there were hosts in the ciborium, and when all the boys had received—most of those present did—there were still as many particles as there were at the beginning.

Word spread quickly among the boys. "Miracle! Miracle! Don Bosco is a saint!" they were saying as they crowded around him after Mass. "Are you sure?" he kept repeating to them, and added: "When you think of it, boys, isn't the Eucharist always a miracle?"

—Peter Rinaldi

Grow!

1. Imagine yourself in the crowd, listening to Jesus' words. In this discourse, what is Jesus promising to you? What is he asking of you or inviting you to do?

   Heart stirred. Who is He? What does it mean to have eternal life? Invitation to a deeper relationship

2. What is your primary focus when you receive the Eucharist? Which of Jesus' promises about the Eucharist speaks to you most deeply? Why? Prayerfully consider whether you could arrange your schedule so that you could receive Communion more frequently.

_____

_____

3. Jesus said, "Those who eat my flesh and drink my blood abide in me, and I in them" (John 6:54). In what ways are you conscious of abiding in Jesus? In what ways do you recognize that he is abiding in you?

_____

_____

_____

_____

_____

_____

4. Many of Jesus' listeners found it difficult to accept his words. Are any of Jesus' statements disturbing to you? If so, why? What could help you accept Jesus' words in faith? What other reactions do you have to Jesus' teaching about himself in John 6:35-59?

_____

_____

_____

_____

_____

5. Peter said, "We have come to believe and know that you are the Holy One of God" (John 6:69). Recalling your own journey of faith, how did you "come to believe and know" that Jesus is the Son of God, your Lord and redeemer?

_____

_____

_____

_____

_____

_____

_____

▶ In the Spotlight
"Holy Communion Makes Me . . . Happy"

For sixteen years, Damien de Veuster (1840–1889), a Belgian missionary priest, served those afflicted with leprosy before dying of the disease himself on the Hawaiian island of Molokai. He was beatified by Pope John Paul II in 1995. On August 26, 1886, Damien wrote this reply to a letter he had received from an Anglican priest, the Reverend Hugh Chapman:

I bless our Lord for having given you, through the example of a poor priest who is merely doing his duty, an understanding of the sweetness of sacrifice. It is the Blessed Sacrament that teaches us how to renounce all human ambition. Without it, I might not have persevered in my resolve to share the lot of the lepers. Now that the expected has come to pass, the effects of leprosy begin to appear on my body. But Holy Communion makes me feel very happy in the somewhat unusual situation in which God has placed me.

—Blessed Joseph Damien de Veuster of Molokai

Reflect!

1. Reflect on these words from Blessed Mother Teresa of Calcutta expressing the intimate relationship Jesus wants to have with us through the gift of himself that he has given to us in the Eucharist, the bread of life:

Jesus made himself the bread of life to satisfy my hunger for him, and he has also made himself the hungry one so that I may satisfy his love for me. He is hungry for us just as we are hungry for him. (*Jesus, the Word to Be Spoken: Prayers and Meditations for Every Day of the Year*)

2. Read and reflect on the following passages to increase your appreciation of the Eucharist and its impact on your life:

A man came from Baal-shalishah, bringing food from the first fruits to the man of God [Elisha]: twenty loaves of barley and fresh ears of grain in his sack. Elisha said, "Give it to the people and let them eat." But his servant said, "How can I set this before a hundred people?" So he repeated, "Give it to the people and let them eat, for thus says the Lord, 'They shall eat and have some left.'" He set it before them, they ate, and had some left, according to the word of the Lord.

—2 Kings 4:42-44

Jesus went to the other side of the Sea of Galilee, also called the Sea of Tiberias. A large crowd kept following him, because they saw the signs that he was doing for the sick. Jesus went up the mountain and sat down there with his disciples. Now the Passover, the festival of the Jews, was near. When he looked up and saw a large crowd coming toward him, Jesus said to Philip, "Where are we to buy bread for these people to eat?" He said this to test him, for he himself knew what he was going to do. Philip answered him, "Six months' wages would not buy enough bread for each of them to get a little." One of his disciples, Andrew, Simon Peter's brother, said to him, "There is a boy here who has five barley loaves and two fish. But what are they among so many people?"

Jesus said, "Make the people sit down." Now there was a great deal of grass in the place; so they sat down, about five thousand in all. Then Jesus took the loaves, and when he had given thanks, he distributed them to those who were seated; so also the fish, as much as they wanted. When they were satisfied, he told his disciples, "Gather up the fragments left over, so that nothing may be lost." So they gathered them up, and from the fragments of the five barley loaves, left by those who had eaten, they filled twelve baskets. When the people saw the sign that he had done, they began to say, "This is indeed the prophet who is to come into the world."

—John 6:1-14

[S]ome boats from Tiberias came near the place where they had eaten the bread after the Lord had given thanks. So when the crowd saw that neither Jesus nor his disciples were there, they themselves got into the boats and went to Capernaum looking for Jesus. When they found him on the other side of the sea, they said to him, "Rabbi, when did you come here?" Jesus answered them, "Very truly, I tell you, you are looking for me, not because you saw signs, but because you ate your fill of the loaves. Do not work for the food that perishes, but for the food that endures for eternal life, which the Son of Man will give you."

—John 6:23-27

[I]t is by God's will that we have been sanctified through the offering of the body of Jesus Christ once for all.

—Hebrews 10:10

Jesus Christ gives Himself entirely to us; He unites His Sacred Body with ours; and, by this union, we become one and the same spirit with Him. As the food which we take nourishes our body, so the Holy Eucharist is the nourishment of our soul. For even as our bodily food is changed into our substance, so the Holy Eucharist transforms us into Jesus Christ.
—St. John Baptist de la Salle

[W]hy should Jesus so ardently desire us to receive him in holy communion? It is because love always sighs for, and tends to a union with, the object beloved. True friends wish to be united in such a manner as to become only one. The love of God for us being immense, he destined us to possess him not only in heaven, but also here below, by the most intimate union, under the appearance of bread in the Eucharist. It is true we do not see him; but he beholds us, and is really present; yes, he is present in order that we may possess him and he conceals himself, that we may desire him, and until we reach our true homeland Jesus Christ wishes in this way to be entirely ours, and to be perfectly united to us.
—St. Alphonsus Liguori

Act!

This week spend some time in adoration before the Blessed Sacrament. Recall these words of Pope Benedict XVI as you are present to Jesus and he is present to you:

[Eucharistic] adoration means saying: "Jesus, I am yours. I will follow you in my life, I never want to lose this friendship, this communion with you." I could also say that adoration is essentially an embrace with Jesus in which I say to him: "I am yours, and I ask you, please stay with me always." (Catechetical meeting with children who had received their First Communion during the year, 15 October 2005)

▶ ## In the Spotlight
Contemporary Voices

"From this time many of his disciples turned back and no longer went about with him" [John 6:66].

Should they have understood? Hardly. It is inconceivable that at that time anyone could have grasped intellectually the meaning of these words. But they should have believed. They should have clung to Christ blindly, wherever he led them. They should have sensed the divine depth behind his words, known that they were being directed toward something unspeakably huge, and simply said: We do not understand; show us what you mean! Instead they judge, everything closes to them. . . .

The Lord demands a clearcut decision also from those closest to him. He is ready to dismiss his last followers if they fail: "Jesus therefore said to the Twelve, 'Do you also wish to go away?'" It is Peter who answers: "Lord, to whom shall we go? Thou hast words of everlasting life, and we have come to believe and to know that thou art the Christ, the Son of God." It is beautiful to see how Peter replies. He does not say: We understand what you mean, but: We hold fast to your hand. Your words are words of life; whether we understand them or not. At that moment, it was the only answer possible.

—Romano Guardini

The Sacrament of Our Salvation

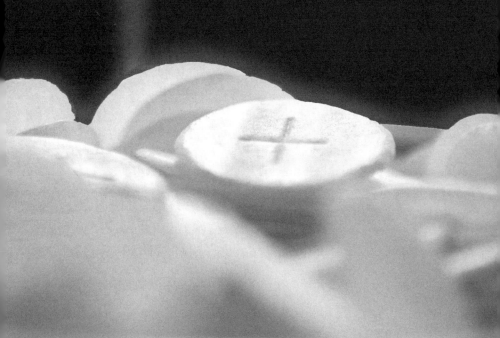

Luke 22:7-20

[7] Then came the day of Unleavened Bread, on which the Passover lamb had to be sacrificed. [8]So Jesus sent Peter and John, saying, "Go and prepare the Passover meal for us that we may eat it." [9]They asked him, "Where do you want us to make preparations for it?" [10]"Listen," he said to them, "when you have entered the city, a man carrying a jar of water will meet you; follow him into the house he enters [11]and say to the owner of the house, 'The teacher asks you, "Where is the guest room, where I may eat the Passover with my disciples?"' [12]He will show you a large room upstairs, already furnished. Make preparations for us there." [13]So they went and found everything as he had told them; and they prepared the Passover meal.

[14] When the hour came, he took his place at the table, and the apostles with him. [15]He said to them, "I have eagerly desired to eat this Passover with you before I suffer; [16]for I tell you, I will not eat it until it is fulfilled in the kingdom of God. [17]Then he took a cup, and after giving thanks he said, "Take this and divide it among yourselves; [18]for I tell you that from now on I will not drink of the fruit of the vine until the kingdom of God comes." [19]Then he took a loaf of bread, and when he had given thanks, he broke it and gave it to them, saying, "This is my body, which is given for you. Do this in remembrance of me." [20]And he did the same with the cup after supper, saying, "This cup that is poured out for you is the new covenant in my blood." (See also Matthew 26:17-19, 26-29 and Mark 14:12-17, 22-25)

> Communion at the table of the Lord reveals and nourishes the friendship Jesus wants to live with us. It is a gift of his love and a sign of his desire to dwell in us all the time.
>
> —Jean Vanier, *Drawn into the Mystery of Jesus through the Gospel of John*

On the first Passover, the night of the ancient Israelites' deliverance from Egypt, God directed them to sprinkle the blood of a lamb on the lintel and doorposts of their houses: "For I will pass through the land of Egypt that night, and I will strike down every firstborn in the land of Egypt, both human beings and animals; on all the gods of Egypt I will execute judgments: I am the LORD. The blood shall be a sign for you on the houses where you live: when I see the blood, I will pass over you, and no plague shall destroy you when I strike the land of Egypt" (Exodus 12:12-13). To this day, Passover is still celebrated among devout Jews each year as "a day of remembrance" just as God had commanded: "throughout your generations you shall observe it as a perpetual ordinance" (12:14).

Jesus made careful preparation to celebrate the Passover with his apostles (Luke 22:7-13). As they gathered to share this meal together, Jesus pointed to his coming passion, telling them, "I have eagerly desired to eat this Passover with you before I suffer" (22:15). This was indeed his last supper with his closest friends, and on this evening before his death, he left them the tremendous gift of the Eucharist. As Pope Benedict XVI vividly described Jesus' own Passover,

> On that night, Jesus goes out and hands himself over to the betrayer, the destroyer, and in so doing, overcomes the night of evil. Only in this way is the gift of the Eucharist, instituted in the Upper Room, fulfilled: Jesus truly gives his Body and his Blood. Crossing over the threshold of death, he becomes living Bread, true manna, endless nourishment for eternity. (Homily, Solemnity of Corpus Domini, 26 May 2005)

When Jesus offered the cup of wine to his apostles, he told them, "This cup that is poured out for you is the new covenant in my blood" (Luke 22:20). His words of consecration echo those spoken by Moses at Sinai, when the blood of the animal sacrifice was sprinkled on the Israelites to consecrate them as God's holy people and to ratify his covenant with them. However, now it is Jesus himself, not a bull or lamb, who is the sacrificial victim, offering his own lifeblood as the atonement for the sins of all humanity and sealing with us a new covenant—the covenant of our redemption.

Each Mass is a repetition of what Jesus taught the apostles to do in his memory (Luke 22:19). In the Mass, we recall Jesus' Passover for us—our deliverance

What songs of thanks and praise we'll sing in the age to come when we eat and drink with Christ at his table in the Father's eternal kingdom!

through his death and resurrection—and celebrate the redemption he won for us on Calvary. But more than simply memorializing his actions, the Eucharist makes Jesus and his sacrificial death actually present to us. The proclamation of faith after the consecration highlights this reality: "When we eat this bread and drink this cup, we proclaim your death, Lord Jesus, until you come in glory." In the New Testament, "proclaim"—in Greek, *katangello*—refers to a public announcement or proclamation (*evangel*) of the Lord's death, of the gospel, of the good news of our salvation (see 1 Corinthians 11:26).

The Eucharist is a sacrifice of praise as well as the sacrament of our salvation. The celebration of the Eucharist is also an act of thanksgiving to God. In fact, the Greek verb *eucharisteo* (Luke 22:19; 1 Corinthians 11:24) means "to give thanks" and "recall[s] the Jewish blessings that proclaim—especially during a meal—God's works: creation, redemption, and sanctification" (*Catechism of the Catholic Church*, 1328; see also 1360). Jesus' meal on the eve of his death also "anticipates the wedding feast of the Lamb in the heavenly Jerusalem" (CCC, 1329). What songs of thanks and praise we'll sing in the age to come when we eat and drink with Christ at his table in the Father's eternal kingdom (see Luke 22:16)!

Understand!

1. What does Luke's account of the Last Supper suggest to you about Jesus' relationship with his apostles? About the importance of the Eucharist to the individual Christian? About its significance within the life of the whole church?

_____

_____

_____

_____

_____

_____

_____

2. In what sense was the Last Supper a meal of fellowship? A sacrificial meal? (It is noteworthy that the "table" of the Eucharist where we share a meal in communion with one another is also an "altar" of sacrifice.)

_____

_____

_____

_____

_____

_____

_____

3. What new meaning did Jesus introduce into the Jewish Passover meal when he departed from the way the rituals and blessings were celebrated by Jews? What do Jesus' actions at the Last Supper add to your understanding of redemption and its price?

_____

_____

_____

_____

_____

_____

_____

4. Why do you think Jesus told his apostles, "Do this in remembrance of me" (Luke 22:19)? How is the eucharistic liturgy more than a mere recollection or memorial meal? What does Jesus' command suggest to you about the institution of the priesthood?

_____

_____

_____

_____

_____

_____

5. Jesus gave thanks, broke the bread, and distributed it to the apostles (Luke 22:19), the same actions that are recounted at the multiplication of the loaves and fish (Mark 6:41). What, in your opinion, is the significance of each of these actions?

_____

_____

_____

_____

_____

_____

Why did Our Blessed Lord use bread and wine as the elements of this Memorial? First of all, because no two substances in nature better symbolize unity than bread and wine. As bread is made from a multiplicity of grains of wheat, and wine is made from a multiplicity of grapes, so the many who believe are one in Christ. Second, no two substances in nature have to suffer more to become what they are than bread and wine. Wheat has to pass through the rigors of winter, be ground beneath the Calvary of a mill, and then subjected to purging fire before it can become bread. Grapes in their turn must be subjected to the Gethsemane of a wine press and have their life crushed from them to become wine. Thus do they symbolize the Passion and Sufferings of Christ, and the condition of Salvation, for Our Lord said unless we die to ourselves we cannot live in Him. A third reason is that there are no two substances in nature which have more traditionally nourished man than bread and wine. In bringing these elements to the altar, men are equivalently bringing themselves. When bread and wine are taken or consumed, they are changed into man's body and blood. But when He took bread and wine, He changed them into Himself.

—Archbishop Fulton J. Sheen

Grow!

1. Jesus and his disciples made careful preparations for their celebration of the Passover meal. How do you prepare yourself to participate at Mass and receive Christ's body and blood in a meaningful way? What could you do to refresh or enhance your appreciation of the Mass if it has become routine to you?

_____

_____

_____

_____

_____

_____

_____

_____

2. Think of an occasion when you felt that Christ particularly touched you or transformed you through your reception of the Eucharist. In what areas of your life do you recognize the effects or see the fruits of receiving Christ's body and blood sacramentally?

_____

_____

_____

_____

_____

_____

_____

3. What do the images of "broken" bread and the cup "poured out" (Luke 22:19-20) add to your understanding of Christ's sacrifice for you? In what ways are these images mirrored in your own life?

_____

_____

_____

_____

_____

_____

_____

4. How is your life a proclamation of the good news of the deliverance and salvation that you have experienced through Jesus' death and resurrection?

_____

_____

_____

_____

_____

_____

_____

5. Recall a time when you were very conscious that your Communion was an act of thanksgiving to God. How could you express your gratitude to God for the gift of the Eucharist in a concrete way?

_____

_____

_____

_____

_____

_____

_____

▶ In the Spotlight
From the *Catechism of the Catholic Church*

From the time of the Mosaic law, the People of God have observed fixed feasts, beginning with Passover, to commemorate the astonishing actions of the Savior God, to give him thanks for them, to perpetuate their remembrance, and to teach new generations to conform their conduct to them. In the age of the Church, between the Passover of Christ already accomplished

once for all, and its consummation in the kingdom of God, the
liturgy celebrated on fixed days bears the imprint of the newness
of the mystery of Christ. (1164)

By celebrating the Last Supper with his apostles in the course
of the Passover meal, Jesus gave the Jewish Passover its defini-
tive meaning. Jesus' passing over to his father by his death and
Resurrection, the new Passover, is anticipated in the Supper
and celebrated in the Eucharist, which fulfills the Jewish Passover and anticipates the final Passover of the Church in the
glory of the kingdom. (1340)

Reflect!

1. Reflect on the sacramental priesthood in the church as a sharing
   in the priesthood of Christ himself. In Christ's place, the priest
   offers us the body and blood that were given for our salvation. As
   the *Catechism of the Catholic Church* explains, "The ministerial
   priesthood has the task not only of representing Christ—Head of
   the Church—before the assembly of the faithful, but also of acting in the name of the whole Church when presenting to God the
   prayer of the Church, and above all when offering the Eucharistic
   sacrifice" (1552).

   Pray for your parish priests and for vocations to the priesthood.
   In what other ways can you support the priests you know?

2. Reflect on the following passages to deepen your understanding
   of the sacrificial lamb as a type and prefigurement of Jesus:

   > The Lord said to Moses and Aaron in the land of Egypt:
   > This month shall mark for you the beginning of months;
   > it shall be the first month of the year for you. Tell the

whole congregation of Israel that on the tenth of this month they are to take a lamb for each family, a lamb for each household. If a household is too small for a whole lamb, it shall join its closest neighbor in obtaining one; the lamb shall be divided in proportion to the number of people who eat of it. Your lamb shall be without blemish, a year-old male; you may take it from the sheep or from the goats. You shall keep it until the fourteenth day of this month; then the whole assembled congregation of Israel shall slaughter it at twilight. They shall take some of the blood and put it on the two doorposts and the lintel of the houses in which they eat it. They shall eat the lamb that same night; they shall eat it roasted over the fire with unleavened bread and bitter herbs. . . . This is how you shall eat it: your loins girded, your sandals on your feet, and your staff in your hand; and you shall eat it hurriedly. It is the passover of the LORD. For I will pass through the land of Egypt that night, and I will strike down every firstborn in the land of Egypt, both human beings and animals; on all the gods of Egypt I will execute judgments: I am the LORD. The blood shall be a sign for you on the houses where you live: when I see the blood, I will pass over you, and no plague shall destroy you when I strike the land of Egypt.

—Exodus 12:1-8, 11-13

[John the Baptist] saw Jesus coming toward him and declared, "Here is the Lamb of God who takes away the sin of the world!"

—John 1:29

For our paschal lamb, Christ, has been sacrificed. Therefore let us celebrate the festival, not with the old yeast, the yeast of malice and evil, but with the unleavened bread of sincerity and truth.

—1 Corinthians 5:7-8

Then I [John] saw between the throne and the four living creatures and among the elders a Lamb standing as if it had been slaughtered. . . . He went and took the scroll from the right hand of the one who was seated on the throne. When he had taken the scroll, the four living creatures and the twenty-four elders fell before the Lamb, each holding a harp and golden bowls full of incense, which are the prayers of the saints. They sing a new song:
> "You are worthy to take the scroll
> and to open its seals,
> for you were slaughtered and by your blood you
> ransomed for God
> saints from every tribe and language and people
> and nation."

—Revelation 5:6-9

▶ In the Spotlight
Meal of Fellowship, Meal of Sacrifice

At a meal where they ate a sacrificial lamb that taught them about divine redemption, Jesus spoke about his body that would be eaten and his blood that would be poured out. He provided the lead concepts that would show the connection with his redemptive death on Good Friday. In a setting where love, forgiveness, and fellowship were experiences as prominent as the theme of sacrifice, Jesus taught that the Breaking of the Bread and the Drinking of the Cup were essentially bound with Christian love and community. Thus the Last Supper was inexorably tied to the building of Christian community and the redemptive sacrifice of Jesus. It was both a fellowship and sacrificial event.

—Alfred McBride, OPraem

Act!

When you attend Mass this week, recall your own personal "Passover"; that is, the times and ways in which you have experienced deliverance from bondage to sin. Offer your Communion as a thanksgiving for this freedom and salvation.

▶ In the Spotlight
The Most Sacred Mystery of the Eucharist

At the Last Supper, on the night he was betrayed, our Savior instituted the eucharistic sacrifice of his Body and Blood. This he did in order to perpetuate the sacrifice of the Cross throughout the ages until he should come again, and so to entrust to his beloved Spouse, the Church, a memorial of his death and resurrection: a sacrament of love, a sign of unity, a bond of charity, a paschal banquet in which Christ is consumed, the mind is filled with grace, and a pledge of future glory is given to us.

—*The Constitution on the Sacred Liturgy*

The Power
of the Cross

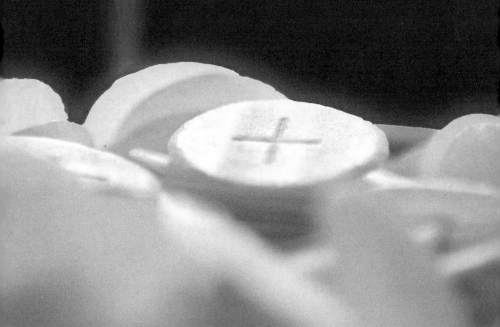

John 19:14-19, 25-37

14 Now it was the day of Preparation for the Passover; and it was about noon. [Pilate] said to the Jews, "Here is your King!" 15They cried out, "Away with him! Away with him! Crucify him!" Pilate asked them, "Shall I crucify your King?" The chief priests answered, "We have no king but the emperor." 16Then he handed him over to them to be crucified.

So they took Jesus; 17and carrying the cross by himself, he went out to what is called The Place of the Skull, which in Hebrew is called Golgotha. 18There they crucified him, and with him two others, one on either side, with Jesus between them. 19Pilate also had an inscription written and put on the cross. It read, "Jesus of Nazareth, the King of the Jews." . . .

25 [S]tanding near the cross of Jesus were his mother, and his mother's sister, Mary the wife of Clopas, and Mary Magdalene. 26When Jesus saw his mother and the disciple whom he loved standing beside her, he said to his mother, "Woman, here is your son." 27Then he said to the disciple, "Here is your mother." And from that hour the disciple took her into his own home.

28 After this, when Jesus knew that all was now finished, he said (in order to fulfill the scripture), "I am thirsty." 29A jar full of sour wine was standing there. So they put a sponge full of wine on a branch of hyssop and held it to his mouth. 30When Jesus had received the wine, he said, "It is finished." Then he bowed his head and gave up his spirit.

31 Since it was the day of Preparation, the Jews did not want the bodies left on the cross during the sabbath, especially because that sabbath was a day of great solemnity. So they asked Pilate to have

> The wine of Christ's blood, drawn from the many grapes of the vineyard that he had planted, is extracted in the winepress of the cross. When men receive it with believing hearts, like capacious wineskins, it ferments within them by its own power.
> —St. Gaudentius of Brescia, Sermon

the legs of the crucified men broken and the bodies removed. [32]Then the soldiers came and broke the legs of the first and of the other who had been crucified with him. [33]But when they came to Jesus and saw that he was already dead, they did not break his legs. [34]Instead, one of the soldiers pierced his side with a spear, and at once blood and water came out. [35](He who saw this has testified so that you also may believe. His testimony is true, and he knows that he tells the truth.) [36]These things occurred so that the scripture might be fulfilled, "None of his bones shall be broken." [37]And again another passage of scripture says, "They will look on the one whom they have pierced."

The Evangelist John specifically tells us in his gospel that Jesus was crucified during the period of preparation for the Passover feast (John 19:14) whereas Matthew, Mark, and Luke state that the crucifixion took place after the Passover meal at which Jesus instituted the Eucharist.* The time framework in the fourth gospel clearly implies that by his death Jesus fulfills the Passover. Jesus' sacrifice on the cross replaced the sacrifices of the old law and inaugurated the new covenant in his blood (see Hebrews 9:12-15).

At noon on the Day of Preparation (John 19:14), the priests began to slaughter the Passover lambs in the temple—male lambs without blemish (Exodus 12:5). At that very hour, Pilate handed Jesus over to be crucified although he found no fault in him. Thus, at the same time that the blood of the paschal lambs was being poured out to commemorate the Israelites' deliverance from slavery in Egypt, Jesus' blood was shed on Golgotha. The Passover in Egypt prefigured the deliverance of humanity from sin, death, and Satan through Jesus Christ, whom John the Baptist had called the Lamb of God (John 1:29). His sacrificial death won for us salvation. Indeed, we have been redeemed "not with perishable things like silver or gold, but with the precious blood of Christ, like that of a lamb without defect or blemish" (1 Peter 1:18-19).

John also recorded that Jesus' legs were not broken, as was often done to hasten the death of a crucifixion victim (John 19:32-33, 36; Psalm 34:20). This is another sign that Jesus is the true Passover sacrifice, for the bones of the Passover lambs were not to be broken (see Exodus 12:46; Numbers 9:12).

Finally, John noted that when a lance was thrust into the side of Jesus' dead body, water and blood flowed out (John 19:34). "What wound was ever more health-giving?" St. Augustine wrote. In this flow of blood and water from Jesus' heart, the Fathers of the Church saw an allusion to baptism and the Eucharist. The verse that John quotes from the prophet Zechariah—"They will look on the one whom they have pierced" (12:10)—is followed by a promise of a fountain springing up to purify God's people from sin (13:1). We are cleansed of our sins by the waters of baptism, and in the Eucharist, we drink from the fountain of life flowing from the heart of our crucified redeemer. With these two sacraments, we are mysteriously present at Golgotha and receive the effects of all Christ accomplished there for us.

Jesus' crucifixion is the fulfillment of another important Jewish ritual, the annual Day of Atonement, when the high priest entered into the inner tabernacle with a blood offering to atone for Israel's sins. On Golgotha, Jesus was both the victim and the great high priest bearing the atoning sacrifice of his own blood into the heavenly tabernacle of which the Holy of Holies was only a symbol. As the Letter to the Hebrews notes of Jesus' atonement for us, "[I]t was fitting that we should have such a high priest, holy, blameless, undefiled, separated from sinners, and exalted above the heavens. Unlike the other high priests, he has no need to offer sacrifices day after day, first for his own sins, and then for those of the people; this he did once for all when he offered himself" (Hebrews 7:26-27).

In the celebration of the Mass and the Eucharist, the sacrifice Jesus offered once for all on the cross remains present to us: "As often as the sacrifice of the cross . . . is celebrated on the altar, the work of our redemption is carried out" (*Dogmatic Constitution on the Church*, 3). Through Christ's death and resurrection, we have been reconciled to the Father and come now to the banquet table of the Eucharist as beloved sons and daughters.

Scholars point to the different calendars and variant ways of calculating dates that were used by the Sadducees, Pharisees, and other Jewish groups of Jesus' day as the most likely reason for this discrepancy between the synoptic gospels and the Gospel of John.

Understand!

1. How are the words that Jesus spoke over the cup of wine at the Last Supper—"Drink from it, all of you, for this is my blood of the covenant, which is poured out for many for the forgiveness of sins" (Matthew 26:27-28)—fulfilled on Golgotha? In what ways are the liturgical actions of the Mass similar to the events enacted on Good Friday?

Paschal lambs slaughtered for passover
(Poured Out)

2. The time of Jesus' death corresponded to the time the lambs were sacrificed in the temple. Why is this so significant? How does it deepen your understanding of redemption?

3. Do Jesus' words, "I am thirsty" (John 19:28), suggest anything more than physical thirst to you? If so, how is Jesus' thirst satisfied? What do you think Jesus meant when he said, "It is finished" (19:30)? See John 17:4 as you consider your answer to this question. In what way does this statement express the victory of the cross?

_____

_____

_____

_____

_____

_____

_____

4. Blood and water flowed from the pierced side of Christ (John 19:34). What does this signify? Read 1 John 5:6-12 for additional insight into the meaning of this occurrence.

_____

_____

_____

_____

_____

_____

5. Why, in your opinion, did John the Evangelist make the following declaration: "He who saw this has testified so that you also may believe. His testimony is true, and he knows that he tells the truth" (John 19:35)?

_____

_____

_____

_____

_____

_____

The whole of the Lord's life was directed toward Calvary. The whole of our life should be oriented toward the Eucharistic Celebration. . . . Each time you celebrate the Eucharist, you have the opportunity to stretch out your hands and nail yourself to the cross with Jesus, to drink his bitter chalice to the dregs. There is no place for mere spectators at Eucharist.
—**Cardinal Francis Xavier Nguyen Van Thuan**

The Eucharist is . . . the memorial of the entire Paschal Mystery: the passion, death, descent into hell, Resurrection and Ascension into heaven; and the Cross is the moving manifestation of the act of infinite love with which the Son of God saved humankind and the world from sin and death.
—**Pope Benedict XVI**

Grow!

1. What particular scene in John's account of Jesus' crucifixion speaks most directly to your life or touches you most deeply right now? Why?

_____

_____

_____

_____

_____

_____

_____

2. Jesus died to atone for humankind's sin and reconcile us to God. Think of an instance in which you experienced this reconciliation in a concrete way. What effect did it have on your personal relationship with God?

_____

_____

_____

_____

_____

_____

3. Mary carried the body of Jesus—flesh of her flesh—in her womb and was present at his crucifixion (John 19:25). How does Mary add to your understanding of the Eucharist and your devotion to Jesus' presence in the Blessed Sacrament?

_____

_____

_____

_____

_____

_____

4. Jesus' pierced heart is a profound sign of his love poured out for us. What is your response to such love? What could you do to grow in loving Jesus more deeply?

_____

_____

_____

_____

_____

_____

5. In what area(s) of your life has the power and victory of the cross been especially apparent to you? How has the power of the cross helped you to overcome sin? Write a prayer of praise and gratitude to Jesus for redeeming you by shedding his blood on the cross.

_____

_____

_____

_____

_____

_____

▶ In the Spotlight
From the *Catechism of the Catholic Church*

Because it is the memorial of Christ's Passover, the Eucharist is also a sacrifice. The sacrificial character of the Eucharist is manifested in the very words of institution: "This is my body which is given for you" and "This cup which is poured out for you is the New Covenant in my blood" [Luke 22:19-20]. In the Eucharist Christ gives us the very body which he gave up for us on the cross, the very blood which he "poured out for many for the forgiveness of sins" [Matthew 26:28]. (1365)

The sacrifice of Christ and the sacrifice of the Eucharist are *one single sacrifice:* "The victim is one and the same: the same now offers through the ministry of priests, who then offered himself on the cross; only the manner of offering is different." . . . "In this divine sacrifice which is celebrated in the Mass, the same Christ who offered himself once in a bloody manner on the altar of the cross is contained and is offered in an unbloody manner" [Council of Trent, 1562]. (1367)

Reflect!

1. Through the centuries many artists have depicted Jesus' crucifixion. Choose a painting or other image to help you visualize the scene at Golgotha. Imagine yourself present there and speak to Jesus about his death for you and your gratitude to him. As St. Leo the Great noted, "Whoever wishes to venerate the Passion of the Lord should contemplate Jesus crucified with the eyes of his soul, and in such a way that he identifies his own body with that of Jesus" (Sermon 15 on the Passion).

2. Reflect on the following passages to enhance your understanding of Christ's atoning sacrifice and the power of the cross:

> [T]hough he was in the form of God,
> [Christ Jesus] did not regard equality with God
> as something to be exploited,
> but emptied himself,
> taking the form of a slave,
> being born in human likeness.
> And being found in human form,
> he humbled himself
> and became obedient to the point of death—
> even death on a cross.
> —Philippians 2:6-8

> In [Christ] all the fullness of God was pleased to dwell, and through him God was pleased to reconcile to himself all things, whether on earth or in heaven, by making peace through the blood of his cross.
> —Colossians 1:19-20

[When] you were dead in trespasses and the uncircumcision of your flesh, God made you alive together with him, when he forgave us all our trespasses, erasing the record that stood against us with its legal demands. He set this aside, nailing it to the cross.

—Colossians 2:13-14

[L]et us run with perseverance the race that is set before us, looking to Jesus the pioneer and perfecter of our faith, who for the sake of the joy that was set before him endured the cross, disregarding its shame, and has taken his seat at the right hand of the throne of God.

—Hebrews 12:1-2

▶ In the Spotlight
Heart of Jesus, Our Peace and Reconciliation

Jesus is peace, he is our reconciliation. He was the one who put an end to the enmity which arose after man had sinned, and who reconciled all people with the Father through his death on the cross. On Golgotha Jesus' Heart was pierced by a lance as a sign of his total self-giving, of that sacrificial and saving love with which he "loved us to the end" (John 13:1), laying the foundation of the friendship between God and man. . . .

The Eucharist is the culmination of our peace. In it is accomplished the sacrifice of reconciliation with God and with our brothers and sisters, in it resounds the word of God announcing peace, in it is raised without end the prayer: "Lamb of God, you take away the sins of the world, have mercy on us." In the Eucharist we receive the gift of Christ himself, who offers himself and becomes our peace.

—Pope John Paul II

Act!

Jesus told his followers, "[W]hen you are offering your gift at the altar, if you remember that your brother or sister has something against you, leave your gift there before the altar and go; first be reconciled to your brother or sister, and then come and offer your gift" (Matthew 5:23-24).

Before the next time you attend Mass, examine your personal relationships. If you need to offer forgiveness to anyone or seek forgiveness from anyone, ask Jesus, who forgave even those who crucified him (Luke 23:34), for his grace and help in this reconciliation.

▶ In the Spotlight
Salvation's Price

The Passover is the holiest and most fervently celebrated of all the feasts in the Jewish calendar. The celebration of the feast, whose date is determined in relation to the vernal (spring) equinox, extends over a period of a week. In Jesus' day, the most important of the ritual ceremonies, the sacrifice of the lambs, took place on the fourteenth or fifteenth day of the month of Nisan, the Day of Preparation.

On this day, Jewish householders brought unblemished yearling lambs—chosen at the markets approved by the Jewish Sanhedrin—to the temple in Jerusalem. At the Levites' signal—three ceremonial blasts blown on their trumpets—the sacrificial offering of the Passover lambs began. This great slaughter was called "preparing the Passover." As each lamb was slain, the priests collected the blood and poured it out before the altar, and the entrails and the fat were burned. After these rituals were completed, the sacrificed lambs—wrapped in their skins—were taken away by their owners to be eaten at the Passover meal.

Jesus was condemned to death and crucified on Golgotha while the Passover lambs were slaughtered in the temple. "The message which Jesus had sought to give the world came at that moment to its consummation," wrote biblical historian Henri Daniel-Rops in *Jesus and His Times*. "Many times he had said that the price of salvation was blood; now that price was paid. . . . Israel was at the very moment absorbed in its rites—at the very moment when these rites were to change in meaning."

The Breaking of the Bread

Luke 24:13-35

[13] Now on that same day two of them were going to a village called Emmaus, about seven miles from Jerusalem, [14]and talking with each other about all these things that had happened. [15]While they were talking and discussing, Jesus himself came near and went with them, [16]but their eyes were kept from recognizing him. [17]And he said to them, "What are you discussing with each other while you walk along?" They stood still, looking sad. [18]Then one of them, whose name was Cleopas, answered him, "Are you the only stranger in Jerusalem who does not know the things that have taken place there in these days?" [19]He asked them, "What things?" They replied, "The things about Jesus of Nazareth, who was a prophet mighty in deed and word before God and all the people, [20]and how our chief priests and leaders handed him over to be condemned to death and crucified him. [21]But we had hoped that he was the one to redeem Israel. Yes, and besides all this, it is now the third day since these things took place. [22]Moreover, some women of our group astounded us. They were at the tomb early this morning, [23]and when they did not find his body there, they came back and told us that they had indeed seen a vision of angels who said that he was alive. [24]Some of those who were with us went to the tomb and found it just as the women had said; but they did not see him." [25]Then he said to them, "Oh, how foolish you are, and how slow of heart to believe all that the prophets have declared! [26]Was it not necessary that the Messiah should suffer these things and then enter into his glory?" [27]Then beginning with Moses and all the prophets, he interpreted to them the things about himself in all the scriptures.

> Whenever the Church celebrates the Eucharist, the faithful can in some way relive the experience of the two disciples on the road to Emmaus: "their eyes were opened and they recognized him."
> —**Pope John Paul II**, *On the Eucharist in Its Relationship to the Church*

²⁸ As they came near the village to which they were going, he walked ahead as if he were going on. ²⁹But they urged him strongly, saying, "Stay with us, because it is almost evening and the day is now nearly over." So he went in to stay with them. ³⁰When he was at the table with them, he took bread, blessed and broke it, and gave it to them. ³¹Then their eyes were opened, and they recognized him; and he vanished from their sight. ³²They said to each other, "Were not our hearts burning within us while he was talking to us on the road, while he was opening the scriptures to us?" ³³That same hour they got up and returned to Jerusalem; and they found the eleven and their companions gathered together. ³⁴They were saying, "The Lord has risen indeed, and he has appeared to Simon!" ³⁵Then they told what had happened on the road, and how he had been made known to them in the breaking of the bread.

It was as Jesus broke the bread with the two disciples in Emmaus that they finally recognized him as their risen Lord. Among Jews, this gesture was typically used to commence the eating of an ordinary meal. Certainly Jesus performed this common practice each day when he ate with his disciples. However, he also invested this gesture with special meaning: the "breaking of bread" is the expression with which the first Christians described the eucharistic liturgy (Acts 2:42, 46; 20:7).

The structure of the eucharistic liturgy as it has been celebrated from the days of the early church mirrors that of the Emmaus episode. On the road to Emmaus, Jesus explained the Scriptures to Cleopas and his companion, presenting to them an overview of salvation history and showing how his entire life—his birth, messianic identity and mission, redemptive death, and resurrection—was foretold by the prophets (Luke 24:25-27). Then, after their hearts had been prepared by this "unfolding" of the word of God, Jesus sat at table with the two disciples and blessed and broke the bread and gave it to them, a sequence of actions recalling the multiplication of the loaves (9:16) and the Last Supper (Luke 22:19; Matthew 26:26). Similarly, at Mass Jesus gives himself to us both in word and in sacrament as we hear the Scriptures proclaimed and receive his body and blood in Communion. Indeed, it is through the proclamation of God's word and the breaking of the bread that the risen Lord remains present with us and with the whole church.

> It is in receiving Christ's body and blood that we can abide in him and he in us.

Luke frequently used the Greek verb *dianoigo* in his gospel and in the Acts of the Apostles. In its most literal sense, this word means "to open something that is shut" in order to gain access into it or passage through it—for example, a closed door or sealed container.

Even a womb is said to be opened in giving birth (Luke 2:23 RSV), and the heavens were opened when Stephen beheld a vision of the Son of Man at the right hand of God (Acts 7:56). Yet *dianoigo* can also be used metaphorically. Thus, when Luke wrote of the Emmaus travelers that "their eyes were opened" (Luke 24:31), he did not mean that they gained visual sight by physically opening closed eyelids. Rather, they experienced supernatural revelation and insight and an inner awareness to recognize Jesus spiritually. And when Jesus opened the Scriptures to the two disciples, he did not unroll a scroll to show what was written on it, but imparted to their hearts a burning spiritual understanding of God's word (24:32). Luke again used *dianoigo* when he told how Jesus opened the minds of the apostles in Jerusalem to comprehend the meaning of the Scriptures (24:46) and how the Lord opened Lydia's heart to listen eagerly to Paul's preaching about Jesus (Acts 16:14).

In the request that Cleopas and his companion made to Jesus—"Stay with us," which also means "abide"—we hear echoes of Jesus' words to his disciples in the Gospel of John (15:4-10): "Abide in me as I abide in you." Although Jesus vanished from their physical sight at the moment the disciples recognized him in faith, his abiding presence remained with them, indeed, even in them—and remains with and in us, too—through the Eucharist. It is in receiving Christ's body and blood that we can abide in him and he in us.

Finally, when the disciples recognized Jesus, they returned excitedly to Jerusalem to tell the other apostles of his resurrection from the dead. We too are called to share the good news of Jesus: "How very significant is the bond between the Church's mission and the Eucharist. . . . Whoever receives Christ in the reality of his Body and Blood cannot keep this gift to himself, but is impelled to share in courageous witness to the Gospel" (Pope Benedict XVI, Angelus Address, 23 October 2005).

Understand!

1. Why do you think Cleopas and his companion failed to recognize Jesus (Luke 24:16) and were "slow of heart" (24:25) to believe?

_____

_____

_____

_____

_____

_____

2. What do Jesus' interactions with the two disciples reveal to you about his character? Choose three adjectives to describe Jesus based on how this story recounts his actions.

_____

_____

_____

_____

_____

_____

3. What does the Emmaus episode suggest to you about the role of Scripture in the life of the church? In your own personal life? What connections do you see here between God's word and faith? Between God's word and the Eucharist?

_____

_____

_____

_____

_____

_____

4. Describe the changes—physical, emotional, and spiritual—that occurred in the two disciples during the course of their encounter with Jesus. What precipitated each of these changes?

_____

_____

_____

_____

_____

_____

_____

5. Why, in your opinion, did Jesus vanish immediately after the disciples recognized him (Luke 24:31)?

_____

_____

_____

_____

_____

_____

▶ In the Spotlight
Contemporary Voices

We must not simply celebrate the Eucharist. We must live the Eucharist or, to put it better, our celebration of the Eucharist should be carried out into our daily lives.

So it was with the two disciples when their eyes were opened after Jesus had broken the bread and handed it to them, "They set out that instant and returned to Jerusalem" (Luke 24:33) to tell their story and with the other disciples to be witnesses for Christ. . . .

We live the Eucharist in our lives if from the Mass we "Go to love and to serve the Lord," to love Him in Himself and in others, to serve Him in others. . . . Each one of us could well reflect in the presence of Christ in the Blessed Sacrament, which is the continuation of the Mass, how we can do this in the particular circumstances of our daily lives, beginning with our own family life.

—Bishop Patrick Walsh

Grow!

1. Recall a time when you failed to recognize Jesus' presence in a situation. What blinded you to his presence? Your own preconceived ideas? Complacency? Intellectual doubt? Something else?

_____

_____

_____

_____

_____

_____

2. The two disciples were drawn together by their shared experiences of grief, of hearing the word of God proclaimed, of table fellowship. How have you been drawn nearer to those in your parish? When do you experience the deepest sense of community and communion with other Christians?

_____

_____

_____

_____

_____

_____

3. Think of an occasion when your heart "burned" within you as you listened to a particular Scripture reading at Mass. How did this word affect your life? If listening to the readings at Mass has been dry or routine to you, what could you do to increase your expectation that God will open his word to you there?

_____

_____

_____

_____

_____

_____

_____

4. How has this study enhanced your appreciation for the Eucharist? What could you do to grow in your love for Jesus present in the Eucharist?

_____

_____

_____

_____

_____

_____

5. When have you shared the good news of Jesus' resurrection and the joy of receiving Jesus in the Eucharist with someone? What hinders you from being more open with others about your faith and its impact on your life?

_____

_____

_____

_____

_____

_____

▶ In the Spotlight
How Close You Are, My Jesus!

Lord Jesus, you are in the Eucharist. You are there, a yard away in the tabernacle. Your body, your soul, your human nature, your divinity, your whole being is there, in its twofold nature. How close you are, my God, my Savior, my Jesus, my Brother, my Spouse, my Beloved!

You were not nearer to the Blessed Virgin during the nine months she carried you in her womb than you are to me when you rest on my tongue at Holy Communion. You were not closer to the Blessed Virgin and St. Joseph in the caves at Bethlehem or the house at Nazareth or during the flight into Egypt, or at any moment of that divine family life than you are to me at this moment and so many others—in the tabernacle. St. Mary Magdalene was no closer to you when she sat at your feet at Bethany than I am here at the foot of this altar. You were no nearer to your apostles when you were sitting in the midst of them than you are to me now, my God. How blessed I am!
—Venerable Charles de Foucauld

Reflect!

1. "It is significant that the two disciples on the road to Emmaus . . . recognized [Jesus] at table through the simple gesture of the "breaking of bread," noted Pope John Paul II in his apostolic letter *Stay with Us, Lord.* "When minds are enlightened and hearts are enkindled, signs begin to 'speak.' The Eucharist unfolds in a dynamic context of signs containing a rich and luminous message. Through these signs the mystery in some way opens up before the eyes of the believer."

Gestures and signs can have a very powerful impact on us. In addition to those related to the Eucharist, what other gestures and signs enhance your personal relationship with the Lord and add more expressive dimensions to it?

2. Read and reflect on the following passages that describe the breaking of bread as experienced in the early church and the unity and community established by sharing the Eucharist:

> [Those] who welcomed [Peter's] message were baptized, and that day about three thousand persons were added. They devoted themselves to the apostles' teaching and fellowship, to the breaking of bread and the prayers. . . . All who believed were together and had all things in common; they would sell their possessions and goods and distribute the proceeds to all, as any had need. Day by day, as they spent much time together in the temple, they broke bread at home and ate their food with glad and generous hearts, praising God and having the goodwill of all the people. And day by day the Lord added to their number those who were being saved.
>
> —Acts 2:41-42, 44-47

> On the first day of the week . . . we met to break bread.
>
> —Acts 20:7

> The cup of blessing that we bless, is it not a sharing in the blood of Christ? The bread that we break, is it not a sharing in the body of Christ? Because there is one bread, we who are many are one body, for we all partake of the one bread.
>
> —1 Corinthians 10:16-17

For I [Paul] received from the Lord what I also handed on to you, that the Lord Jesus on the night when he was betrayed took a loaf of bread, and when he had given thanks, he broke it, and said, "This is my body that is for you. Do this in remembrance of me." In the same way he took the cup also, after supper, saying, "This cup is the new covenant in my blood. Do this, as often as you drink it, in remembrance of me." For as often as you eat this bread and drink the cup, you proclaim the Lord's death until he comes.

—1 Corinthians 11:23-26

▶ In the Spotlight
The Celebration of the Eucharist

From a second-century account of the basic order of the eucharistic celebration:

On Sunday we have a common assembly of all our members, whether they live in the city or in the outlying districts. The recollections of the apostles or the writings of the prophets are read, as long as there is time. When the reader has finished, the president of the assembly speaks to us; he urges everyone to imitate the examples of virtue we have heard in the readings. Then we all stand together and pray.

On the conclusion of our prayer, bread and wine and water are brought forward. The president offers prayers and gives thanks to the best of his ability, and the people give their assent by saying, "Amen." The Eucharist is distributed, everyone present communicates, and the deacons take it to those who are absent. . . .

We hold our common assembly on Sunday because it is the first day of the week, the day on which God put darkness and

chaos to flight and created the world, and because on that
same day our savior Jesus Christ rose from the dead.
—St. Justin Martyr

Act!

This week, bake or buy a special loaf of bread and share it at a meal
with your family or friends. Pay attention to the life-giving quali-
ties of the bread and how it nourishes and unites you as you eat it
together.

▶ In the Spotlight
Communion Creates Community

Communion with Christ is also communion with us. . . . A
Christian is not a person isolated from the rest of the world or
one who walks alone. The disciples returning to Emmaus were
two . . . and a third wayfarer joined them. So a small community that walked with Christ was formed.

At the end of the route the two disciples shared the same
experience: "Were not our hearts burning (within us) while
he spoke to us on the way and opened the scriptures to us?"
The hearts of those two disciples spiritually became one. Christ
places us in a communion of feelings, thoughts and wishes. . . .

The disciples from Emmaus slowly acquired one heart to
the extent that they walked with the Lord and if one walks
with Christ, a little at a time one establishes a relationship
"with his Body" and one becomes one body with him.
—Igor Kowalewski

Practical Pointers for Bible Discussion Groups

A Bible discussion group is another key that can help us unlock God's word. Participating in a discussion or study group—whether through a parish, a prayer group, or a neighborhood—offers us the opportunity to grow not only in our love for God's word but also in our love for one another. We don't have to be trained Scripture scholars to benefit from discussing and studying the Bible together. Bible-study groups provide environments in which we can worship and pray together and strengthen our relationships with other Christians. The following guidelines can help a group get started and run smoothly.

Getting Started

- Decide on a regular time and place to meet. Meeting on a regular basis allows the group to maintain continuity without losing momentum from the previous discussion.

- Set a time limit for each session. An hour and a half is a reasonable length of time in which to have a rewarding discussion on the material contained in each of the sessions in this guide. However, the group may find that a longer time is even more advantageous. If it is necessary to limit the meeting to an hour, select sections of the material that are of greatest interest to the group.

- Designate a moderator or facilitator to lead the discussions and keep the meetings on schedule. This person's role is to help preserve good group dynamics by keeping the discussion on track. He or she should help ensure that no one monopolizes the session and that each person—especially shy or quiet individuals—is offered an opportunity to speak. The group may want to ask members to take turns moderating the sessions.

- Provide enough copies of the study guide for each member of the group, and ask everyone to bring a Bible to the meetings. Each session's Scripture text and related passages for reflection are printed in full in the guides, but you will find that a Bible is helpful for looking up other passages and cross-references. The translation provided in this guide is the New Revised Standard Version: Catholic Edition. You may also want to refer to other translations—for example, the New American Bible or the New Jerusalem Bible—to gain additional insights into the text.

- Try to stay faithful to your commitment and attend as many sessions as possible. Not only does regular participation provide coherence and consistency to the group discussions, it also demonstrates that members value one another and are committed to sharing their lives with one another.

Session Dynamics

- Read the material for each session in advance and take time to consider the questions and your answers to them. The single most important key to any successful Bible study is having everyone prepared to participate.

- As a courtesy to all members of your group, try to begin and end each session on schedule. Being prompt respects the other commitments of the members and allows enough time for discussion.

If the group still has more to discuss at the end of the allotted time, consider continuing the discussion at the next meeting.

- Open the sessions with prayer. A different person could have the responsibility of leading the opening prayer at each session. The prayer could be a spontaneous one, a traditional prayer such as the Our Father, or one that relates to the topic of that particular meeting. The members of the group might also want to begin some of the meetings with a song or hymn. Whatever you choose, ask the Holy Spirit to guide your discussion and study of the Scripture text presented in that session.

- Contribute actively to the discussion. Let the members of the group get to know you, but try to stick to the topic, so that you won't divert the discussion from its purpose. And resist the temptation to monopolize the conversation, so that everyone will have an opportunity to learn from one another.

- Listen attentively to everyone in the group. Show respect for the other members and their contributions. Encourage, support, and affirm them as they share. Remember that many questions have more than one answer and that the experience of everyone in the group can be enriched by considering a variety of viewpoints.

- If you disagree with someone's observation or answer to a question, do so gently and respectfully, in a way that shows that you value the person who made the comment, and then explain your own point of view. For example, rather than say, "You're wrong!" or, "That's ridiculous!" try something like, "I think I see what you're getting at, but I think that Jesus was saying something different in this passage." Be careful to avoid sounding aggressive or argumentative. Then, watch to see how the subsequent discussion unfolds. Who knows? You may come away with a new and deeper perspective.

- Don't be afraid of pauses and reflective moments of silence during the session. People may need some time to think about a question before putting their thoughts into words.

- Maintain and respect confidentiality within the group. Safeguard the privacy and dignity of each member by not repeating what has been shared during the discussion session unless you have been given permission to do so. That way everyone will get the greatest benefit out of the group by feeling comfortable enough to share on a deep, personal level.

- End the session with prayer. Thank God for what you have learned through the discussion, and ask him to help you integrate it into your life.

The Lord blesses all our efforts to come closer to him. As you spend time preparing for and meeting with your small group, be confident in the knowledge that Christ will fill you with wisdom, insight, and grace and the ability to see him at work in your daily life.

Sources and Acknowledgments

INTRODUCTION

Pages 13–14:
Bernardo Olivero, *The Search for God: Conferences, Letters, and Homilies* (Kalamazoo, MI: Cistercian Publications, 2002), 134.

Page 14:
Ignatius of Loyola, quoted in *The Voice of the Saints,* selected and arranged by Francis W. Johnston (Rockford, IL: Tan Books and Publishers, Inc., 1986), 89–90.

SESSION 1: MANNA IN THE DESERT

Page 17:
John Paul II, Homily at Wroclaw Cathedral, Poland, 31 May 1997, www.vatican.va/holy_father/john_paul_ii/travels/ documents/hf_jp-ii_hom_31051997_en.html. © Libreria Editrice Vaticana. Used with permission.

Page 23:
Bede the Venerable, Commentary on the First Letter of Peter, quoted in *The Liturgy of the Hours,* vol. II (New York: Catholic Book Publishing Co., 1976), 705. Excerpt from the English translation of Non-Biblical Readings from *The Liturgy of the Hours* © 1974, International Committee on English in the Liturgy, Inc. (ICEL). All rights reserved. Used with permission.

Catechism of the Council of Trent, Section 3: "The Sacrament of the Eucharist," www.catholicapologetics.info/ thechurch/catechism/Holy7Sacraments-Eucharist.shtml.

Page 25:
Theophane Vénard, quoted in *The Voice of the Saints*, selected and arranged by Francis W. Johnston (Rockford, IL: Tan Books and Publishers, Inc., 1986), 92.

Pius X, quoted in Bert Ghezzi, *Voices of the Saints: A Year of Readings* (New York: Doubleday, 2000), 614.

André Bessette, quoted in Rosemary Ellen Guiley, *The Quotable Saint* (New York: Checkmark Books, 2002), 34.

Page 29:
Augustine, quoted in *The Voice of the Saints*, 91.

Ambrose, On the Mysteries, Nn. 43, 47-49, quoted in *The Liturgy of the Hours*, vol. III (New York: Catholic Book Publishing Co., 1975), 507-508. Excerpt from the English translation of Non-Biblical Readings from *The Liturgy of the Hours* © 1974, International Committee on English in the Liturgy, Inc. (ICEL). All rights reserved. Used with permission.

SESSION 2: THE BLOOD OF THE COVENANT

Page 31:
Francis Xavier Nguyen Van Thuan, *The Road of Hope: A Gospel from Prison* (Boston: Pauline Books & Media, 2001), 81. English Language Edition Copyright ©

Daughters of St. Paul. Used by permission of Pauline Books & Media, 50 St. Paul's Avenue, Boston, MA 02130. All rights reserved.

Page 38:

Thomas Aquinas, *Summa Theologica*, III, 75, 1, www.ccel .org/a/aquinas/summa/TP/TP075.html#TPQ75OUTP1.

John Vianney, quoted in *The Voice of the Saints*, selected and arranged by Francis W. Johnston (Rockford, IL: Tan Books and Publishers, Inc., 1986), 89.

Pages 41–42:

Walter J. Ciszek, *He Leadeth Me* (San Francisco: Ignatius Press, 1995), 126–127. Used with permission of Ignatius Press.

Page 42:

Anima Christi, quoted in Manuel Ruiz Jurado, SJ, *For the Great Glory of God: A Spiritual Retreat with St. Ignatius* (Ijamsville, MD: The Word Among Us Press, 2002), 46.

Page 43:

Ambrose, On the Sacraments, quoted in Jill Haak Adels, *The Wisdom of the Saints: An Anthology* (New York: Oxford University Press, 1987), 82.

Cyril of Alexandria, Homily 142, quoted in R. Payne Smith, *A Commentary on the Gospel according to St. Luke by St. Cyril, Patriarch of Alexandria* (New York: Studion Publishers, Inc., 1983), 570.

Session 3: Jesus' Revelation

Page 45:

Ignatius of Antioch, Letter to the Romans, quoted in *The Liturgy of the Hours,* vol. III (New York: Catholic Book Publishing Co., 1975), 329. Excerpt from the English translation of Non-Biblical Readings from *The Liturgy of the Hours* © 1974, International Committee on English in the Liturgy, Inc. (ICEL). All rights reserved. Used with permission.

Pages 50–51:

Peter Rinaldi, *Man with a Dream: The Story of Saint John Bosco* (New Rochelle, NY: Salesiana Publishers, 1997), 69–70. Used with permission of Salesiana Publishers.

Page 53:

Joseph Damien De Veuster, quoted in Omer Engelbert, *Damien: Hero of Molokai* (Boston: St. Paul Books & Media, 1994), 183.

Page 54:

Mother Teresa of Calcutta, *Jesus, the Word to Be Spoken: Prayers and Meditations for Every Day of the Year,* compiled by Brother Angelo Devananda (Servant Books, 1986), 71. Used with permission of St. Anthony Messenger Press. www.AmericanCatholic.org. All rights reserved.

Page 56:

John Baptist de la Salle, quoted in *The Voice of the Saints,* selected and arranged by Francis W. Johnston (Rockford, IL: Tan Books and Publishers, Inc., 1986), 88.

Alphonsus Liguori, *The Love of Our Lord Jesus Christ Reduced to Practice*, chapter 2, quoted in *The Navarre Bible: The Gospel of St. John*, with a commentary by the members of the Faculty of Theology of the University of Navarre (Blackrock, Ireland: Four Courts Press, 1995), 106.

Pages 56–57:
Benedict XVI, Catechetical meeting with children who had received their First Communion during the year, 15 October 2005, www.vatican.va/holy_father/benedict_xvi/ speeches/2005/october/documents/hf_ben_xvi_spe _20051015_meeting-children_en.html. © Libreria Editrice Vaticana. Used with permission.

Page 57:
Romano Guardini, *The Lord*, 240. Copyright © 1982. Published by Regnery Publishing, Inc. All rights reserved. Reprinted by special permission of Regnery Publishing, Inc., Washington, DC.

Session 4: The Last Supper

Page 59:
Jean Vanier, *Drawn into the Mystery of Jesus through the Gospel of John* (Mahwah, NJ: Paulist Press, 2004), 129.

Page 60:
Benedict XVI, Homily at the Mass and Eucharistic Procession on the Solemnity of Corpus Domini, 26 May 2005, www.vatican.va/holy_father/benedict_xvi/homilies/2005/ documents/hf_ben-xvi_hom_20050526_corpus-domini _en.html. © Libreria Editrice Vaticana. Used with permission.

Page 64:
Fulton J. Sheen, *Life of Christ* (New York: Image Books/ Doubleday, 1990), 278.

Pages 69–70:
Alfred McBride, *To Love and Be Loved by Jesus: Meditation and Commentary on the Gospel of Mark* (Huntington, IN: Our Sunday Visitor Publishing Division, 1992), 127. The permission to reproduce copyrighted materials for use was extended by Our Sunday Visitor, 200 Noll Plaza, Huntington, IN 46750. 1-800-348-2440. Web site: www.osv.com. No other use of this material is authorized.

Page 70:
The Constitution on the Sacred Liturgy, 4 December 1963, no. 47, *Vatican Council II: The Conciliar and Post Conciliar Documents,* vol. I, ed. Austin Flannery, OP (Northport, NY: Costello Publishing Company, 1998), 16.

Session 5: The Crucifixion

Page 73:
Gaudentius of Brescia, Sermon, quoted in *The Liturgy of the Hours,* vol. II (New York: Catholic Book Publishing Co., 1976), 670. Excerpt from the English translation of Non-Biblical Readings from *The Liturgy of the Hours* © 1974, International Committee on English in the Liturgy, Inc. (ICEL). All rights reserved. Used with permission.

Page 75:
Augustine, quoted in Richard T. A. Murphy, *Days of Glory: The Passion, Death, and Resurrection of Jesus Christ* (Ann Arbor, MI: Servant Books, 1980), 136.

Page 76:
Dogmatic Constitution on the Church, 21 November 1964, no. 3, *Vatican Council II: The Conciliar and Post Conciliar Documents,* vol. I, ed. Austin Flannery, OP (Northport, NY: Costello Publishing Company, 1998), 351.

Page 79:
Francis Xavier Nguyen Van Thuan, *The Road of Hope: A Gospel from Prison* (Boston: Pauline Books & Media, 2001), 77. English Language Edition Copyright ©, Daughters of St. Paul. Used by permission of Pauline Books & Media, 50 St. Paul's Avenue, Boston, MA 02130. All rights reserved.

Benedict XVI, Angelus Address, 11 September 2005, www.vatican.va/holy_father/benedict_xvi/angelus/2005/documents/hf_ben-xvi_ang_20050911_en.html. © Libreria Editrice Vaticana. Used with permission.

Page 82:
Leo the Great, Sermon 15 on the Passion, quoted in Francis Fernandez, *In Conversation with God – Volume Two* (London: Scepter Ltd., 1989), 232.

Page 83:
John Paul II, Address at Devotion to the Sacred Heart of Jesus, 7 June 1999, no. 2, www.catholic-forum.com/saints/pope0264xp.htm. © Libreria Editrice Vaticana. Used with permission.

Page 85:
Henri Daniel-Rops, *Jesus and His Times,* vol. 2 (Garden City, NY: Image Books/Doubleday, 1958), 222.

Page 87:
John Paul II, On the Eucharist in Its Relationship to the Church, 17 April 2003, no. 6, www.vatican.va/holy_father/ special_features/encyclicals/documents/hf_jp-ii_enc _20030417_ecclesia_eucharistia_en.html. © Libreria Editrice Vaticana. Used with permission.

Page 90:
Benedict XVI, Angelus Address, 23 October 2005, www.vatican.va/holy_father/benedict_xvi/angelus/2005/ documents/hf_ben-xvi_ang_20051023_en.html. © Libreria Editrice Vaticana. Used with permission.

Page 92–93:
Patrick Walsh, 2005 Lenten Pastoral Letter, Diocese of Down and Connor, Northern Ireland, 21 February 2005, www.downandconnor.org/default2.asp?active_page_id=192. Used with permission of the Most Reverend Patrick Walsh, Diocese of Down and Connor, Northern Ireland.

Page 95:
Charles de Foucauld, *The Spiritual Autobiography of Charles de Foucauld,* ed. and annotated by Jean-François Six (Ijamsville, MD: The Word Among Us Press, 2003), 98.

John Paul II, *Stay with Us, Lord,* Apostolic Letter for the Year of the Eucharist, 7 October 2004, no. 14, www.vatican .va/holy_father/john_paul_ii/apost_letters/documents/hf_jp-ii_apl_20041008_mane-nobiscum-domine_en.html. © Libreria Editrice Vaticana. Used with permission.

Pages 97–98:

Justin Martyr, *First Apology in Defense of the Christians,* quoted in *The Liturgy of the Hours,* vol. II (New York: Catholic Book Publishing Co., 1976), 695. Excerpt from the English translation of Non-Biblical Readings from *The Liturgy of the Hours* © 1974, International Committee on English in the Liturgy, Inc. (ICEL). All rights reserved. Used with permission.

Page 98:

Igor Kowalewski, *On Christ, the Eucharist, and the Road to Emmaus,* videoconference address sponsored by the Vatican Congregation for Clergy, Moscow, 18 March 2005, www.catholic.org/featured/headline.php?ID=1926.

Also in The Word Among Us Keys to the Bible Series

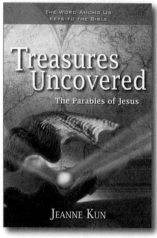

Item# BTWAE5

Treasures Uncovered: The Parables of Jesus
A Six-Week Bible Study for Catholics
by Jeanne Kun

This popular six-session Scripture guide will help you explore the surprising—and often challenging—dimensions of six of Jesus' parables. Fascinating historical details, explanations of the Greek root words used in the original gospels, and quotations from church fathers included.

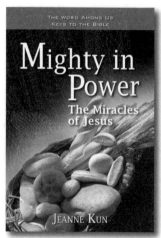

Item# BTWBE6

Mighty in Power: The Miracles of Jesus
A Six-Week Bible Study for Catholics
by Jeanne Kun

This Scripture guide will help you understand the miracles of Jesus as invitations to experience God's mercy and salvation today. Each of the six sessions includes questions for delving into the miracles of Jesus and applying them to daily life. Suitable for individuals or groups.

To order call 1-800-775-9673 or order online at www.wordamongus.org